S0-ATK-312

BOSTON'S FIRST NEIGHBORHOOD:

The North End

by Paula J. Todisco

BOSTON PUBLIC LIBRARY

Cover photography and design by Richard Zonghi

Printing by the Boston Public Library Duplicating Department

Copyright 1976
by the Trustees of the Public Library
of the City of Boston

Funded in part by the Massachusetts Bureau of Library Extension with a special project grant to public libraries from the Library Services and Construction Act, Title I.

Library of Congress Cataloging in Publication Data

Todisco, Paula J   1950-
  Boston's first neighborhood.

  Bibliography: p.
  1. North End, Boston. 2. Minorities—Massachusetts—Boston—History.
3. Boston—History. I. Title.
F73.68.N65T62   974.4'61   76-10292
ISBN 0-89073-009-1

Contents

Introduction

The North End is people. People in adversity, people in prosperity. People in happy times, people facing tragedy. People in a community, working together; individuals working alone. It is people growing, eating, dreaming, celebrating, fighting, singing, dying, living. For over 300 years, since Boston was founded, the North End has been there, always filled with the movement, the laughter, the tears, and the aspirations of people. A long time — 300 years — a very long time.

In the following history many institutions are named, many firsts are chronicled, many events of great historic importance are included. Yet the backbone of North End history is the people who built it, changed it, and who lived out their lives in its narrow, twisted streets. From the first Puritan to the latest Italian immigrant, the history of the North End is really the history of the people who have lived there.

The North End has served a unique function in Boston. It was a springboard for the settlement of Boston in Puritan years. Later it became a center of commerce in the growing city. After a crucial role in the development of the American Revolution, the North End seemed to sink into obscurity. In reality, it was simply changing one vital role for another. It became one of the great entry points for the immigrant masses. Through the North End's ancient streets passed many who arrived as poor, uneducated foreigners, yet who lived to see themselves and their children become successful in a new land. Irish, Jews, Portuguese, Italians: waves of immigrants have descended upon the North End and the North End has absorbed them and sheltered them. Countless Bostonians and other Americans today might be surprised to discover ancestors who lived in the North End at some time in their lives.

This chronicle will endeavor to capture some of the excitement of many divergent streams of humanity passing through the North End and to indicate the unique position of the district as a point of entry to the new world for countless generations of new Americans. The North End symbolizes for Americans of all nationalities the common experience that nearly all of our ancestors faced. As each new immigrant arrived, often destitute, often ill, perhaps discouraged and overwhelmed, he saw the spire of the Old North Church rising aloft, a visible encouragement. The spire reminded the weary traveler that other Americans before him had come from across the seas to struggle and to succeed in forming a new country. These people, great and small, are the North End's story.

Now is a good time to look back across the centuries, reaching beyond the events of 200 years ago, already recalled in this bicentennial year, to see where the North End has been and to determine where it may be headed. This exploration shows us that the North End's strength has been in the people who have lived here and cherished the area as their home. People will continue to be the strength of the North End if the community is to grow in the days ahead.

Acknowledgments

Thanks are due to a number of people without whose help this history could not have been undertaken:

To John Dexter of the North Bennet Street Industrial School for the loan of his scrapbooks.

To Pietrina Maravigna for articles from her private files.

To the staff of the North End Branch Library — Barbara Cordaro, Sister Mary Bergazzi, and Rhonda Massie — for their full cooperation.

To Geraldine Herrick, Branch Librarian, for her comments and encouragement.

To Jane Manthorne, Coordinator of Young Adult Services, for her many editorial suggestions and for her enthusiasm about the project which made revising it a pleasant task.

To the North End Community at Large.

The friendliness and kindness of all have made this a memorable year for the author.

NORTH-END FOREVER.

Tho.ˢ Moore's Lithog.ᵞ Boston.

HULL STREET GUARDS

QUICK STEP,

Composed & respectfully dedicated to the

OFFICERS & MEMBERS OF THE **H. S. GUARDS**,

BY

JOHN HOLLOWAY,

Performed for the first time by the
Boston Brass Band at their parade,
June 15.ᵗʰ 1838.

Boston · Pub.ᵈ by H.PRENTISS, N.º 2 Pemberton Hill.

Chapter One
PURITANS AND REVOLUTIONARIES
1630 to 1775

The North End is the oldest residential district in Boston. A solitary English pastor, Rev. William Blackstone, seems to have been the first European to occupy any part of the area now thought of as the North End. He retains a certain distinction in being possibly the only person ever to view a quiet North End as he gazed out at the peninsula from his home near Louisburg Square. He was not allowed to remain at peace for long, however. John Winthrop and an enterprising band of Puritans arrived near the site of the Charlestown Bridge in 1630 and quickly set about establishing houses near Spring Lane. This first settlement was near the present Dock Square. With the construction of the Central Artery in the 1950's, Dock Square became isolated from what is now considered North End; but in colonial Boston, Dock Square was very much a part of the area. The Puritans' arrival there meant the end of solitude in the North End, and poor pastor Blackstone soon moved on to more promising (in his view) pastures.

At that time the North End was quite noticeably different in physical size and shape from its present-day configuration. Ann Pollard, arriving with Winthrop's band as a child of 12, has left this not very appealing description of the area: it was a "place very uneven, abounding in small hollows and swamps covered with blueberries and other small bushes."[1] A large tidal inlet, later known as Mill Pond, was one of the more prominent features of the landscape. When a causeway was built, roughly paralleling present-day Causeway Street, a large segment of the North End — extending inland to Salem and North Margin Streets — was covered with shallow water. Low marshes in the area of Blackstone Street were channeled by the erection of a dam into Mill Creek. This actually severed the North End physically from the rest of Boston during the colonial period. The North End's separateness was emphasized by its colonial epithet, the "Island of North Boston."[2] Thus, from the earliest days of Boston's history, both physical and social conditions have served to make North Enders feel distinct from, even though part of, the developing community of Boston. In addition to Mill Creek, Copp's Hill was the other outstanding physical feature, being somewhat higher in 17th-century Boston than it is now. Along with parts of Beacon Hill, the top was sheared off to fill Mill Pond later in the colonial period.

Whatever the advantages or disadvantages of the site, it obviously met with Winthrop's approval and the settlers proceeded quickly to

1

Map of the Colonial North End by William Burgiss

establish their homes. The first houses (small, thatched-roof buildings surrounded by pasture and garden areas) were pretty much scattered willy-nilly, clustering around the area of North Square and North Street. This haphazard arrangement helped create the narrow streets, winding alleys, and secluded places which still characterize the North End. In 1636 streets in Boston's North End were among the first to be officially designated as streets. The outlines of streets we now know as North, Hanover, and Salem appeared then much as they remain today. At that time North Street was known as Ann Street, Fish Street, and Ship Street. Hanover bore the names of Middle, Hanover, and North (causing some confusion with present-day North Street), and parts of Salem Street were designated Back Street and Green Lane.

In addition to gardening and keeping livestock, the early settlers often engaged in various crafts, working out of their homes. Shoemaking, carpentry, and shipbuilding are representative of the early trades practiced in Puritan Boston. The early settlers soon established the patterns of hard work and frugality that have characterized so many of the North Enders through the centuries. They were staunchly religious, sober, God-fearing people who had left England to establish a home — and a state — based on their religious principles.

Naturally, the establishment of a suitable place of worship was important to them, and in 1650 the Second Church of Boston, also known as the North Church or Old North Church, was established in North Square. Churches proliferated in the North End throughout the colonial period as groups developed new tenets and sought institutions through which to express them. This constant forming and re-forming of belief shows how vitally important religion was to the early settlers. Puritan ministers, in fact, were so influential in colonial affairs that probably the most significant name in early North End history was that of a famous family of divines, the Mathers. Through their ministry at the Second Church, they exerted a profound influence on the history of not only the North End, but all of New England.

The family's history in the New World begins with Richard Mather who came to Dorchester in 1635 and was a minister there until his death in 1689. A leader of Congregationalism, he, in collaboration with Rev. Thomas Welde and Rev. John Eliot, produced the famous Bay Psalm Book.

His son Increase, born in 1639, achieved even greater fame and with it a measure of controversy. Increase was graduated from Harvard College in 1656 and became associated with the Second Church in 1664. He was elected president of Harvard College in 1681, but believing his duty to his congregation outweighed his desire to be an educator, declined the invitation. He was later persuaded to serve from 1684 until 1701, when pressure to choose between the demands of Harvard and his own church led him to resign from Harvard in favor of his ministry in the North End church.

Increase became deeply involved with the colonists' struggles to preserve their original charter. Granted by Charles I at the time the colony was founded, the Charter of the Massachusetts Bay Colony was very favorable to the settlers. Aware that the charter freed the Puritans from much royal control, the British demanded its return in 1634. The independent Puritan colonists did not wish to give up a document that granted them so many liberties, however. Tradition has it that the charter was hidden in a house on what was afterwards called Charter Street to prevent its seizure and revocation. The charter was revoked, nonetheless, in 1684, sparking a grave crisis for the young colony. Increase Mather was in the forefront of those who asserted that the colonists must not submit to the King's wishes. When a formal protest was organized in 1688, Mather was chosen to take church petitions to London for negotiations with the King, then James

II. Because of the opposition of royalist forces in Boston, led by the royal governor, Mather was threatened with arrest and finally forced to begin his diplomatic mission by fleeing the colony in disguise.

While he was in London, the colonists revolted against the Governor, Sir Edmund Andros, on April 18, 1689. By this time James had been succeeded by the Protestant William III, and Increase was able to secure a new compromise charter and suggest a more acceptable governor, William Phips (also a North End resident). While the new charter was not as liberal as the previous one, displeasing some colonists, Mather's negotiations had yielded as favorable a charter as possible.

After his return from the London mission, Increase became involved in the controversial Salem witch trials of 1692, as did his son Cotton. The Mathers supported the witch-finders, and Cotton even effected several "cures" himself in Boston. When the hysteria of the hunt died down, Bostonians in general were uneasy at the excesses committed at the height of the madness. It was not surprising that the Mathers, because of their prominence in the community, were targets of the adverse reactions to the persecutions. Some of Increase's other later ideas were not popular either, particularly his farsighted interest in smallpox inoculation; but at the time of his death in 1723, grieving parishioners fully mourned him for the leadership he had displayed through the years.

Cotton Mather continued the family tradition, attending Boston Latin School and Harvard College. At the age of 12, he was the youngest student ever enrolled at Harvard. After graduation he joined his father in the church in North Square where he was ordained in 1685. He was connected with this church for the rest of his life. Cotton wished to succeed his father as president of Harvard College. To his great disappointment, this dream was never realized, but he later was offered the presidency of Yale. As with his father, insinuations about his involvement in the witch trials of 1692 were damaging to his popularity. Cotton was a prodigious author and his *Magnalia Christi Americana*, perhaps more than anything else, has assured his place in history.

The last Mather preacher, Cotton's son Samuel (1706-1785), attended North Grammar School and followed the family tradition by graduating from Harvard in 1723 and becoming pastor at the Second Church in 1731. His wife Hannah was the sister of Thomas Hutchinson, later a royal governor of Massachusetts. Hutchinson, like his predecessor Edmund Andros, achieved a high degree of unpopularity. Samuel himself did not seem to enjoy as much popularity as his forbears in the church, and in 1741 doctrinal differences with Rev. Joshua Gee and charges of improper conduct led to his dismissal from the Second Church. He subsequently founded the 10th Congregational Church on the corner of North Bennet and Hanover Streets with 93 of the 353 parishioners of the Second Church. Following his death, the church passed to Rev. John Murray and became the First Universalist Church. The dynasty of Mather preachers was over after 150 years. The Puritan heyday in the North End and indeed throughout Massachusetts was also at an end. Despite the wishes of the divines of Boston, prosperity brought an interest in worldly goods, and North Enders were hardly immune to the temptations of earthly wealth, even with their strict religious heritage. The solid, sober, God-fearing craftsmen of the earliest North End community had been, in large measure, replaced by a more worldly, more fashionable breed.

Tracing the history of the Mathers has taken us beyond the 17th century, yet there were other North Enders whose lives serve to illustrate the temper of that early community. Sir William Phips, the royal governor nominated by Increase Mather, typifies the resourcefulness of the North Ender. Although born in Maine (one of 26 children), he began his career as an apprentice to a ship's carpenter in the North End. Phips' ambition to acquire sufficient wealth to build a fine mansion in the North End was realized when he recovered a sunken treasure ship on one of his sea voyages. For his efforts Phips was awarded not only the treasure, which made him a rich man, but a knighthood. He was able at last to return to the North End and build a magnificent house on the corner of Charter and Salem (then known as Green) Streets. This mansion was known as the "fair brick house in the Green Lane of Boston."[3] Unfortunately, Phips' term as governor was marred by the witchcraft hysteria in 1692.

In order to maintain rapid expansion in the 17th century, a community such as the North End naturally had to develop not only sufficient produce to sustain itself, but methods to refine and convert that produce into its most useful form. Not surprisingly then, the establishment of mills was an early consideration for North End settlers. As one might expect, Mill Creek was used as one source of water power for the milling operations. The natural operation of the wind was another. On July 31, 1643, Henry Symonds (or Simmons), John Bulton, and others were granted all the land between the town cove and the marshes beyond to erect "one or more Corne Mills, and mayneteyne the same forever."[4] (At that early time corn was legal tender in the colonies.) This was the first windmill in the colony, and what could be more appropriate than to name the land surrounding it Windmill Hill or Mill Hill or Mill's Field. Other mills, including sawmills and chocolate mills, soon followed the establishment of this first mill. Within 20 years of the founding of the colony, a gristmill stood at the head of the Mill Pond dam, and a sawmill where the canal joined Mill Pond. Eventually, Windmill or Mill Hill was also called Snow Hill after a street in London and, finally, Copp's Hill, the name by which it is known today.

One inevitable result of the settlement of an area is the need for a cemetery. The first cemetery in Boston was established around King's

Copp's Hill Burial Ground, final resting place of many prominent North Enders

Chapel, or, rather, King's Chapel was built at the site where many settlers had been buried. It was not long before the number of prospective patrons would have led to severe overcrowding of the cemetery, and town fathers began the search for a second suitable location. As a result, land was purchased from John Baker and Daniel Turrell on Copp's Hill, the most prominent location in the North End, on February 20th, 1659, and part of Copp's Hill became the North Burying Ground. The hill had been named for William Copp, a shoemaker who plied his trade on Prince Street, and gradually the cemetery also became known by his name. The cemetery was subsequently enlarged by the addition of land belonging to Judge Samuel and Hannah Sewall in 1708. There were several other additions, including one in 1809, which made Copp's Hill — 88,000 square feet — the largest cemetery in the city proper. The fame of the burial ground is assured, not only for its antiquity, but because it is the repository of so many noteworthy personages. Cotton, Samuel, and Increase Mather are all buried there. The father and grandfather of Gov. Thomas Hutchinson rest in Copp's Hill as well. Edmund Hartt, builder of the *USS Constitution;* Andrew and John Eliot, two well-known ministers; Deacon Shem Drowne, artisan of weather vanes; and Capt. Robert Newman, who achieved a footnote in history for hanging the lanterns in the Old North Church as a signal to Paul Revere — all are among the notables who reside in the burying ground. No wonder it was known also as "Corpse Hill." The grave of Prince Hall, founder of the African Masonic Grand Lodge of Massachusetts, is also here. It serves as a reminder that over 1,000 slaves and freedmen are also buried in the cemetery, many of them former residents of Boston's first black district, located in the North End. Known as "New Guinea," the black community was located at the foot of Copp's Hill on the Snow Hill Street side. On the southerly side a man named Stanley kept pasture. He achieved note as the first person in Boston to bequeath property to the public schools.

There were three points at the Copp's Hill end of the North End: Windmill or Wheeler's Point, Ye Mylne Point or Hudson's Point at Charter and Commercial Streets, and Merry's Point at the east corner of the North End. There, around 1643-44, a fortification was erected known as the North Battery. The name later became associated with Battery Wharf. Obviously, the early colonists felt the need to protect themselves from attackers, especially those coming from the sea. Hudson's Point received its name from Francis Hudson, innkeeper and ferryman. The first regular ferry to Charlestown, vitally important to the colonists as a means of transportation and communication, was begun on May 6, 1635, from this point. The absence of a ferry would have meant a much longer journey down river for the northbound traveler.

The North End at this time was a healthy place in which to live; but the early settlers, in common with the inhabitants of today and throughout the long history of the North End, had to fear that ancient enemy, fire. North Square, at that time the center of North End life, containing the Mathers' church and a thriving marketplace, was demolished in a particularly vicious conflagration in 1676. Under the leadership of Increase Mather, the church was quickly rebuilt. A house, owned by Paul Revere nearly 100 years later, was built shortly thereafter (c. 1680) on the North Street site of the Mathers' old homestead, which also had been destroyed in the blaze. (Before the Mathers, the site was occupied by an unfortunate Capt. Kemble who was punished for what was deemed the lewd and lascivious behavior of kissing his wife in public on the Sabbath day after his return from a long voyage at sea.)

Another large fire destroyed warehouses and mariners' taverns near the docks on August 8, 1679. One realizes how closely-packed houses were when more than 80 dwellings and 70 warehouses were destroyed in one fire in a very small area of the North End. In response to the ever-present fear of fire, which could spread with amazing quickness in an area where all dwellings were wooden and crowded closely together, a Ralph Carter and seven other men combined forces to acquire a fire engine for the North End in 1683. However, another fire, important enough to be noted, occurred in 1691 causing great destruction to an area between the Mill Creek drawbridge and the Mill bridge on Hanover Street.

The early North Enders, except for their random placement of dwellings in the first years of the colony, demonstrated a remarkably orderly and, it would seem, united approach to building a secure and self-sustaining colony in the 17th century. They must have felt an extreme dedication to a common goal to have accomplished so much in the first 50 years. As noted before, success brought change to the colony. Materialism and the ambition for wealth and status grew. London society was imitated in Boston streets. Fashion became more important to both ladies and men. It would be overly harsh to see this as decadence in the society, yet a certain relaxation naturally seems to have accompanied the Puritans' success. In this new, softer climate a more individualistic and independent mind could be allowed to flourish.

One measure of the new spirit was apparent in the proliferation of different religions and the increase of tolerance not only in Boston but in the North End. The Puritan church began to lose its supremacy as other religions founded congregations and older Puritan congregations split over doctrinal differences. One such split was already noted in the ministry of Samuel Mather in 1741. This proliferation became extreme enough to cause some confusion for the researcher today in sorting out the different churches of the 17th and 18th centuries. Yet examples of religious ferment serve to illustrate how North Enders were perceiving their world.

As indicated above, the Second Church, where the Mathers held sway, was founded in 1650 in North Square. For 64 years it was the *only* church in the North End, and was also known as the New Meeting House and the North Meeting House. Later on it also received the appellation "Old North." (The practice of applying several names to many of the buildings and streets in colonial times and to switch names can lead to confusion for modern researchers.) The Second Church was quickly rebuilt after the Great Fire of 1676 and continued its ministry until 1775 when it was torn down for fire wood by the British occupying Boston. In 1714 a church called the New North was formed on the corner of Clarke and Hanover Streets because of crowding at the Old North Church. Peter Thatcher (for whom Thacher Street is named) was the second minister of this church from 1720-21 to 1738-39. Apparently he also had problems with his congregation, a large segment of which departed in 1719 to organize the New Brick Church. This church was also known as the "Revenge" church, indicating the motivations of the recessionist parishioners of the New North in leaving their church, and the "Cockerel" church because of its large, prominent weathervane, said to be a representation of the unfortunate Rev. Thatcher. The remaining parishioners of the New North, undaunted by the loss of their fellow worshipers, continued to function for many years. After Peter Thatcher, Andrew and then John Eliot served in its pulpit from 1742 until 1813. The Eliots lived in the Hanover Street house owned by the Mathers after they departed from North Square. The Eliots' name is today commemorated by the Eliot School, the oldest grammar school in the United States. During their tenure, the New North's original small wooden building was replaced by a beautiful brick edifice designed by noted architect Charles Bulfinch in 1802.[5] The bells of the church were cast by a North End notable, Paul Revere. Purchased by the Roman Catholics in 1863, the New North was renamed St. Stephen's and today, beautifully restored through the efforts of Cardinal Cushing, is the only Bulfinch church left in Boston. As a Catholic church, its congregation has been Irish, Portuguese, and — finally — Italian.

The New Brick, meanwhile united with the Old North (in North Square) after the latter's demolition in 1775, taking its original name, the Second Church. Ralph Waldo Emerson was one of the many eminent people who preached from its pulpit in the 19th century. The church dissolved in the mid 1800's (1852), the famous weathervane being sold to Cambridge Congregational Church. By this time its Protestant congregation had left the North End, and the church followed, moving to Bowdoin Square.

Samuel Mather's church was given to the Universalists upon his death in 1785. In 1838 it, too, was succeeded by a brick edifice, becoming finally the Baptist Seamen's Bethel. The Baptists had started meetings in 1665 in Charlestown. Their first North End place of worship was near Mill Pond on Back, or Salem, Street in 1679. At Mather's request, most of his parishioners returned to the Second Church after his death.

The Methodists' second house of worship in Boston began services in 1796 on Hanover and North Bennet Streets. A more elaborate structure, dedicated in 1828, has the distinction of having had a unique disaster occur at the opening ceremonies. In the middle of the service the floor collapsed, plunging the assembled congregation into the basement! The building became the Portuguese church of St. John the Baptist in the late 19th century. In 1912 the building was bought by the city of Boston to house the North End Branch Library.

Soon after the New Brick Church was formed, the first Anglican parish was established in the North End. Nothing shows how Puritanism was declining as completely as the spread and growth of the Anglican church which represented all the royal authority, power, and persecution that the early Puritans had fled. King's Chapel, the first Anglican church, had been erected by Governor Andros in 1686 over the objection of local residents who would not sell him land for his church. But only 37 years later there were enough English merchants and crown officials to erect a second Anglican church, Christ Church, popularly known as Old North Church today. The cornerstone was laid on April 15, 1723, with Rev. Samuel Myles of King's Chapel taking as his text, "May the gates of Hell never prevail against it." Thus far, they have not. The church was formally opened on December 29, 1724. The first pastor, Rev. Timothy Cutler, had been president of

Yale College from 1719 until he renounced his Puritan faith in favor of Anglicanism in 1722. His church is now the oldest continuously functioning church in the North End, surviving revolution and social changes that have seen its entire congregation move away from the area.

Christ Church's beautiful building is a copy of a Christopher Wren church in London (destroyed in World War II).[6] Its great beauty lies in its graceful, simple lines uncluttered by needless adornment. In the 18th century the church was both a royal favorite and the recipient of many valuable gifts from the parishioners, so that today there are many beautiful and historic objects in the building. Chief among them is the set of magnificent bells — the first ring of bells in America — cast in England for the church in 1774. Paul Revere, who seems to have been involved in every activity of colonial Boston, was one of the bell ringers at Christ Church. The bells are no longer rung in the old method for fear that the strain will cause the steeple to topple. These fears are well founded because the steeple, first finished in 1740 and 191 feet in height, has had its subsequent ups and downs. It was blown down in 1804 and re-erected in 1807 under the direction of Charles Bulfinch. Forty years later it underwent extensive repairs only to need restoration again in 1912. In 1954 hurricane Carol blew the steeple down for a second time, but it was restored through the donations of many citizens.

King George III sent the silver communion service, prayerbooks, damask cushions, vestments, and the so-called "Vinegar Bible" of 1717. The Bible received its name from the misprinting of the word "Vineyard," from the parable of that name, to "Vinegar." Two brass chandeliers were the gift of Capt. William Maxwell and have graced the interior since before 1735. The candleholders were first lighted on Christmas day in 1724. Deacon Shem Drowne, the colonial artisan, designed the Old North's weathervane which resembles a waving banner. These many beautiful gifts adorn a church which is cited today as one of the finest examples of colonial architecture.

Over 1,000 people are buried in the church's crypt, including Major John Pitcairn, British commander of the expedition to Lexington and Concord, who was fatally wounded at the Battle of Bunker Hill. His body was to have been returned to England to lie in Westminster Abbey; however, a careless sexton sent the wrong body. The mistake was never corrected, and Pitcairn's remains are still in American soil. Samuel Nicholson, the first commander of the *Constitution*, is also buried there.

Christ Church would be a memorable church in any event because of the many important North Enders who have worshipped here throughout its long ministry; but its place in history was assured on that eventful night just over 200 years ago, later memorialized by Henry Wadsworth Longfellow. As every school child knows, "on the

18th of April in '75" Sexton Robert Newman placed two lanterns in the steeple to signal Paul Revere, waiting in Charlestown, that the British would be marching to Concord that night. There has been some controversy in the intervening years about this historical incident. One disputer claims that it was not Robert Newman but a Capt. John Pully, Jr., a friend of Paul Revere, who placed the lanterns in the church steeple. Proponents of this thesis point to Pully's subsequent flight, in disguise, to Cohasset. Newman never seems to have been questioned by the British about the incident.

Another controversy named the Second Church, known at that time as the Old North, as the church from which the lanterns were hung. Supporters of this theory feel that this Old North was not as prominent as Christ Church. They feel that a signal from Christ Church would have been as visible to the British in the harbor as it was to Paul Revere, whereas a lantern in the North Church might have escaped their attention. Paul Revere was a member of the Old North, while Christ Church had many loyalist members among its parishioners. The Old North was demolished by the British shortly thereafter, while Christ Church continued to hold services almost uninterruptedly throughout the war. Despite these claims, including a book written by a pastor of the Second Church when it had become Universalist, Christ Church has continued to be regarded by the majority of experts as the place from which the signal shone.

Today the lights in the steeple of Christ Church still shine forth as a visible reminder to resident and tourist alike of the spirit that spread from the North End to all of the colonies, a symbol of the courage and convictions that animated the men and women who fought for freedom from oppression. Christ Church has looked upon patriot and immigrant equally in their struggles to define and reach their dreams. Fittingly, it still stands, the only building ever erected on this site, a link between the residents of 250 years ago and the Americans of today.

While religion was not the dominant force in the 18th century that it had been in Puritan Boston, the number of thriving churches and the attention accorded to building, furnishing, and preserving houses of worship, such as Christ Church, indicate that the worship of God was still a major force in North End life. However, in the 18th-century world of the North End at least four major influences on the social life of the time are apparent. The four influences are revealed in the building and development of marketplaces, wharves, taverns, and schools. The development of the markets led to the growth of North Square as the social and economic center of the town. Many of the wealthiest citizens established themselves there. The business world no longer focused solely on small crafts, but turned its attention to the wharves where a thriving merchant and shipbuilding business was expanding. Many local taverns were achieving importance not only as places of relaxation and social gathering, but for their role in fostering the spread and development of revolutionary thought that ultimately led to a united opposition to the King. The necessity of education assumed an importance beyond the need to supply a competent ministry to the young colony.

In the earliest years of the colony there was no fixed marketplace. The town was small enough for those with goods to sell and those wishing to buy to be able to locate each other, usually by going door to door. It was not really necessary to have a formal market area. As the colony grew, however, following the custom of Britain, a market day — usually Thursday — was observed. Three temporary structures for a market were erected — one in North Square, one at the site of the Liberty Tree, and one at the Town Dock near the site of Faneuil Hall — over the strenuous opposition of a conservative element which did not see the need for improving the old system.

A market area attracts a congregation of people. North Square thus early became one of the social centers of Boston life. The church was here, the market was here, and soon many prominent families built houses near the square as well. The Mathers, as already noted, had a home on the site of the Paul Revere House. The square was first called Clark Square after a Major Thomas Clarke (spellings vary), a wealthy merchant who built his house there around 1711. His house was later sold to Sir Charles Henry Frankland. Frankland, not only wealthy but knighted, took as ward a young girl from Marblehead named Agnes Surriage to raise and educate. As Agnes grew older her situation in the Frankland household caused a good deal of comment until a lucky accident intervened in her behalf. While touring Portugal in 1753, Sir Henry nearly lost his life in an earthquake and Agnes was credited with his rescue. This seems to have jolted Frankland at last, and Agnes returned home as Lady Frankland! North Square was also known for a time as Frizell Square after John Frizell, another wealthy merchant whose home was on Garden Court Street. Frizell achieved distinction as the first man in the North End to keep a carriage and have a stable, located on Moon Street.

Fashionable living was becoming part of North End life. Garden Court Street was the home of Col. Thomas Hutchinson and of his son Thomas, later the royal governor, until 1765. The Hutchinson family had long been active in public affairs, but adopted a more conservative loyalist viewpoint that made them increasingly unpopular with more radical forces in Boston. On August 26, 1765, a mob protesting the passage of the Stamp Acts ransacked Hutchinson's mansion. Barely escaping the attack upon him, Hutchinson was ever after embittered. His natural feeling that the common crowd was not fit to govern was greatly strengthened by this attack. Later as royal governor, he made himself extremely unpopular by rigidly upholding the authority of the King and Parliament against the revolutionary movements. He died in exile, an unhappy man.

Of course, no catalog of famous North Square residents would be complete without recalling Paul Revere, the patriot whose celebrated midnight ride is known to nearly everyone through Longfellow's poem. Revere was typical of the North End population of the day. He was not as wealthy as Gov. Hutchinson or Sir Charles Henry Frankland or John Frizell, but he was a solidly well-off artisan who supported two wives (in succession) and a total of 16 children. He was also a member of that middle class who were most offended by the restrictive laws passed by Parliament in the years before the Revolution. He was not a Christ Church Anglican as many of the wealthiest were, but he was a member of the Mathers' Congregationalist Second Church. His family were originally Huguenots. The social lines drawn by the religions were not so great that he could not join the bell ringers at Christ Church; yet, broadly speaking, Christ Church members were more apt to be upper-class loyalist supporters of the King. Many of the men who helped fan revolutionary flames were, like Revere, prosperous and usually peaceful businessmen who felt that their economic livelihood was being threatened by a king and a parliament which would not give them an equal say as Englishmen.

Revere undertook many careers in his life: goldsmith, engraver, silversmith, founder of a powder mill in Canton, the second in the colonies, founder in 1783 of a cannon and bell foundry on Foster Street, and in 1795 an organizer of the Charitable Mechanics Association (and first president). Yet today he is almost solely remembered, except by collectors of Paul Revere bowls, for his patriotic endeavors. In the Boston Tea Party of December 16, 1773 his name appears second on the role of participants. One year after the Boston Massacre the event was recalled by a series of illuminations placed in the windows of the Revere House in North Square. The lighted pictures depicted the bloody clash and called for the avenging of the victims' deaths. In the fall of 1774 and winter of 1775 Revere organized a committee for watching the British in Boston. This system of watchers was so effective that within a few hours of the British decision to march to Lexington and Concord, three messengers had alerted Revere. After his historic ride, he was appointed a lieutenant colonel in command of a regiment of militia, but was not much involved in the fighting. His was a full and honorable life of service to the country and his fellow man.

North Square retained its importance throughout the 18th century. Its prominence as a center of commerce was aided by its location. Contemporary visitors would be surprised to note that in 1770 North Square was only one block from the wharves. Centuries of building out and wharving over have extended the shoreline so that many places once near the water are a few blocks inland now. However, visitors today can see how cramped and tiny the triangular square is. It could not serve as the principal marketplace for long.

Boston needed another market and, through good fortune and one man's kindness, a market was erected.

In 1740 Peter Faneuil, having inherited a goodly fortune, offered to pay for the building of a marketplace if the town would agree to maintain it. By 1742 it was completed, with an additional story for use as a town hall. A grateful town voted to name it for the donor, who unfortunately died just after the building was dedicated. A eulogy for Faneuil was the first address delivered in the new hall. Holding over 1,000 people, it was the ideal spot for town meetings and for other gatherings, many of them increasingly revolutionary in tone. Because of its importance as a patriot meeting place, Faneuil Hall has become known as the "Cradle of Liberty." A fire in January of 1761 gutted the building. However, it was reopened in March of 1763. During the occupation of Boston by the British, it was turned into a storehouse for arms and furniture and even used as a theatre by the troops. Again the building was damaged — many portraits were stolen and never recovered — but again it was restored to a place of prominence. Deacon Shem Drowne, whose weathervanes adorned so many buildings of the period, including the Old North and Cockerel Churches, also designed the grasshopper which perches atop Faneuil Hall. Many theories have been advanced as to what the grasshopper represents, but whatever its origins, the grasshopper has become a landmark in its own right. The temporary loss of the grasshopper in 1974 caused much chagrin. When the weathervane was found and placed back on its perch, all Boston breathed a sigh of relief. The market district has continued in the Faneuil Hall, Dock Square, and Blackstone Street area right up to the present day. Thanks in large part to the foresight and generosity of Peter Faneuil, one of Boston's most colorful attractions flourishes at a time when supermarkets and frozen foods have replaced good fresh produce on many American tables.

The twin activities of shipbuilding and merchant operations were meantime constantly expanding along the waterfront. Many of the richest North End families made their money through commerce on the seas and their names are preserved in the wharves from which they sailed. The wealthy Clarke family of North Square owned Clarke's wharf and shipyard, the largest of the time. Here all manner of goods — both legal and illegal — were brought in. Even one of John Hancock's ships was seized here in June 1768 for containing contraband. This action was followed by a colonial riot in which windows were broken and the royal customs officer attacked.

The famous tea party is another example of Bostonian — especially North End — reluctance to let their rules of commercial enterprise be determined by an unsympathetic parliament 3,000 miles away. The tea overturned at Griffin's Wharf was at first destined for the Clarke family warehouses. However, the members of the family were awakened at one o'clock on a November morning in 1773 with demands to turn over the tea when it arrived. A little disturbed by this incident, the family had the tea sent instead to Griffin's Wharf. That certainly did not forestall the colonists one bit from their plan to stop the sale of the tea.

Other famous wharves of the time were Scarlett's Wharf, extending from Fleet Street; Union Wharf, originally known as Vernon's after its owner Captain Fortesque Vernon (1758), then later as Goddard's Wharf and May's Wharf; Gray's Wharf, after the shipowner William Gray; and India Wharf with its Bulfinch-designed warehouses. The ocean commerce made all of Boston prosper, and soon North Enders were sailing all around the world. Capt. Robert Gray, a North Ender, was the first merchant to carry the U. S. flag around the world, discovering the Columbia River and helping claim U. S. control over Oregon. Colorful characters such as Capt. Thomas Gruchy, merchant, shipowner, and reputed smuggler also joined North End society. He moved into the Phips mansion on Charter Street and quickly gained a certain measure of respectability by joining the Old North Church, even serving as a junior warden in 1748. However, despite his posture as a law-abiding citizen, rumor had it that he used a 14-foot tunnel, the remnants of which are still visible at 453 Commercial Street, to smuggle in goods from the wharves. As mysteriously as he arrived, he one day "up and left," taking his treasure with him.

Education has always had a place of importance in Massachusetts. It was only six years after the founding of Boston that it was deemed necessary to begin a college for the education of clergymen, Harvard College. In addition, some schooling in the basics of writing, reading, spelling, and arithmetic was necessary even for those who had no calling to the pulpit. So in 1713 the North Latin School or Grammar School was founded on North Bennet Street. The building was the gift of Capt. Thomas Hutchinson, father of the royal governor. The first master of the school was Recompense Wadsworth. The Latin or Grammar School was annexed to the North Writing School in 1789. The Writing School had been founded in 1718 and stood on Love Lane directly adjoining the Latin School. It was so successful that it finally absorbed the earlier school. The success of the Writing School was proabuly due to its master for more than fifty years, John Tileston. Tileston, who was known as "Master Johnny," was born in the North End on February 27, 1735. At 14 he was apprenticed to Master Zachariah Hicks at the Writing School and served as its head from 1762 to 1819. An active patriot, he was a familiar North End sight in his later years when he still wore the old-style colonial dress. In commemoration of his service to the community, Love Lane became known as Tileston Street. His school continued and was known finally as the Eliot School after the ministers Andrew and John from the New North Church. Today it is the oldest grammar school in the United States and also boasts the oldest alumni association.

Besides being diligent students, the North End boys were also diligent fighters. From early colonial times scrapping among North Enders or with other neighborhoods has been a way to "let off steam." Those who remember Italian-Irish battles across the Charlestown Bridge will be surprised to know that 200 years earlier North End boys and their Charlestown neighbors were engaged in running combat. Within the district Copp's Hillers fought Prince Streeters, and both fought Ann Streeters (North Street). Fights even erupted on the Common between neighborhood groups until stopped by Mayor Quincy. Decorum was not always the order of the day in the North End, even in Puritan times. In addition to combat, the North End boys liked sports. A favorite winter amusement was sledding. Up on Foster Street was Sliding Alley, perfect for such colonial sports. Even today Slide Park remains a recreational area for North End youth.

In an age when newspapers and broadsides were apt to be infrequent and expensive, the North Enders — like colonists everywhere — relied upon local watchmen and the word-of-mouth of travelers and friends for receiving much of their information, not only for that which came from far away, but for local town news and gossip. The taverns provided a convivial spot for exchanging and discussing the news of the day. Throughout the critical period of the 1750's and 60's, as revolutionary thought grew in the minds of North Enders, the local taverns remained centers of the developing organizations of patriots.

One of the oldest inns was the Ship Tavern, also known as "Noah's Ark" due to a fancied resemblance between the ship on its sign and the biblical vessel. Dating back to at least 1650, the tavern dispensed drink and good cheer for over 200 years. The Ship was a favorite resort of the King's commissioners. At one time it belonged to the Hutchinsons and, through Hannah Hutchinson, to Samuel Mather. A seam in the wall was said to be a legacy of an earthquake which struck Boston in 1663. The tavern stood opposite Clarke's Shipyard in a location easily accessible to the many North Enders who worked on the waterfront.

The Red Lion was another famous hostelry of the colonial period. Standing on North and Richmond Streets, it fell victim to the great fire of 1676 but was rebuilt. Recompense Wadsworth, one of the owners, was also the first master of the North Grammar School. Apparently, in colonial days there was room for an enterprising man to be successful in two very different occupations. Henry Wadsworth Longfellow, memorializer of that North End patriot Paul Revere, was a descendant of Recompense. North End descendants are likely to be found anywhere!

The two most famous taverns for those involved in revolutionary activities were Salutation Tavern and the Green Dragon Inn. It was in the Salutation Tavern (also known as the Two Palaverers) that ardent revolutionaries gathered. It, too, had been a meetingplace from the early days of the colony, first opening in 1662; but it was through its patriotic connections that it achieved its historic importance. As noted before, the middle classes of the day — the small businessmen and merchants — were suffering the greatest losses as a result of royal policies. Salutation Alley, near the waterfront on Salutation and North Streets, was a gathering place for the men who worked in ship-building and the other small tradesmen of the area. These men, known as "mechanics," were among the first to argue the merits of liberty and self-government. The Committee on Safety was formed here and plans for the Boston Tea Party originated here also. Finally, it was the spawning ground of the North End Caucus, a revolutionary organization which spied on British movements. Most experts agree that caucus is a corruption of "caulkers," taken from the ship caulkers who were well represented in meetings.[7] All the famous revolutionary Bostonians met here: Sam Adams, James Otis, Joseph Warren, Josiah Quincy, Jr., John Adams, Paul Revere, John Hancock. The Caucus is said to have originated with Joseph Warren who, besides his activities as a teacher and physician, was an active patriot. He was the author of the Suffolk Resolves (a document that foreshadowed the Declaration of Independence), a president of the Provincial Congress, and a casualty at the Battle of Bunker Hill in 1775.

After the Tea Party, Caucus members were obliged to move their activities to the Green Dragon Tavern on Union Street. Their continued plotting caused the Green Dragon to be known as a "nest of treason."[8] Actually, some sources indicate that patriot meetings were occurring there before the Tea Party and that the disguised Indians left from the Dragon. Probably both taverns were influential gathering places throughout this period. The Green Dragon was the unofficial home of the Freemasons of Boston. Revere and others were members of this organization, so it is reasonable to assume that they brought their revolutionary ideas with them to Masons' meetings.

While the colonists were planning revolution in the Green Dragon, close by on Marshall Lane the *Massachusetts Spy*, one of the colonies' early newspapers, was printed. Actually, the *Spy* was first produced on Salem Street in 1770 by Isaiah Thomas in the office of Zachariah Fowle. In 1771 Thomas moved the paper to Marshall Street where, under its motto of "Open to all parties, but influenced by none," it continued publication to 1775. The paper was not as nonpartisan as its motto may lead a person to think, and just before the Battle of Lexington, Thomas felt it expedient to move to Worcester, escaping the worst of the British occupation.

The ride of Paul Revere and the start of the revolution marked a climax in North End history, although the patriots who began the war had no way of knowing it. Until 1775 action critical to the history of the whole American continent had been occurring in the North End through the efforts of these ordinary citizens. However, for the first year of the war the city of Boston remained under British control. While the patriot faction is best remembered in American history, the population of the North End was divided almost into equal camps: the patriots, the loyalists, and those who were prepared to swing either way. With the British occupying their streets and even certain houses, North End patriots had to be extremely discreet if they wished to stay in Boston.

No fighting occurred in Boston at all except for the Battle of Bunker Hill. The North End had a unique vantage point for observing the progress of this battle. From Copp's Hill a clear view could be had of Charlestown. The British wounded were brought back to the North End, including Major Pitcairn who was carried to a house on Prince Street. (Tradition says it was no. 130.) [9] It was said that bloodstains from the wounded and dying British were visible in Prince Street houses for many years after the battle. During the occupation the Green Dragon Tavern became a hospital and the Second Church was torn down. British troops performed plays and were quartered in Faneuil Hall. Christ Church, with its large loyalist congregation, continued to hold services, however. The occupation continued until 1776 when the arrival of cannon from Fort Ticonderoga for installation at Dorchester Heights forced the British generals to the realization that they were in an indefensible position militarily. Their response was to evacuate Boston entirely.

At the lifting of the seige of Boston, the many loyalists in town left with General Howe. Over 1,000 of the North End's most wealthy and influential residents were among them. They became exiles in Canada and England. It is easy to overlook the fact that while Revere, Adams, and others plotted in North End taverns, there were an equal number who remained loyal to the established government, even when its fortunes fell. These loyalists were the people who had given the North End its aura of glamor and fashion.

At the same time as this migration was occurring, the war shifted to the middle and southern states. Boston was no longer the center of revolutionary activity. The North End was out of the spotlight of national affairs. As the wealthy left and mansions were emptied, no one else of equal means appeared to replace them. Until the war, one third of the population of Boston resided in the North End. [10] After 1800, for a variety of reasons, the tide of population growth shifted and the North End felt the change.

Chapter Two
DECLINE AND
THE IRISH IMMIGRATION
1775 to 1880

In the 19th century many of the very factors that made the North End such an attractive place of residence for earlier inhabitants now worked to drive respectable or well-off Bostonians away from the area. The exodus of Loyalists after 1776 only accelerated a trend that would have been felt in the North End sooner or later anyhow. For Boston was expanding in many ways. The wealthy began building homes on Beacon Hill and then in various sections of the Back Bay as these areas were opened to habitation by the leveling and filling operations that went on throughout this century. Eventually, as transportation improved, affluent Bostonians moved out to Roxbury and beyond, seeking to escape the restrictions of city life. Meanwhile, in downtown Boston business and financial empires were being strengthened. The advent of industrialism signaled the end of the smaller artisans with their home-run businesses and crafts which had been prevalent in colonial Boston. Areas of industry were no longer desirable areas in which to live. They were becoming increasingly crowded and noisy.

The North End had always been at the center of the shipping and merchant businesses. Their growth brought more warehouses, more dockyards, more sailors and transients to the area. This created a less desirable neighborhood for the citizen who could afford to live elsewhere. Those who could afford to maintain the great mansions built by previous generations no longer wished to own them. Decline came swiftly for the North End in this period. Within a little more than a generation the old North End families that had remained after the war were leaving. North Street, in particular, sank rapidly into degradation. Hanover and Salem Streets remained a region of small merchants, tradesmen, and artisans ringed by the expanding commercial network. One small drygoods-store owner who began business in the years after the Loyalists fled was Eben Jordan, whose store was at 168 Hanover Street. After a merger with Mr. Marsh's business, the operation flourished as Jordan Marsh Company, still a famous name in New England.[1] However, successful business enterprises such as Mr. Jordan's are almost the only bright note for the North End of the early 19th century.

Different sources list different families as the last to leave the North End, but the Dodd family and Lyman Beecher's family seem to have been among those reluctant to move.[2] Sheafe Street in general was a bastion of the old aristocrats; but left isolated in a sea of deterioration, they soon made a swift exodus.

One of the most dilapidated areas of the North End in the early part of the century was Webster Avenue. Narrow and dark, the street — little more than a passageway between houses — was inhabited at that time chiefly by black families. In wealthier days Capt. John Manley, the first naval officer appointed by George Washington, had lived there. Much of the housing was wiped out during a celebration of the end of the war of 1812. Apparently, the jubilant residents lighted candles in their windows to signify their happiness at the war's end. Then they went out to observe the festivities in other areas of the town. The unattended candles soon burned down and began a conflagration that meant catastrophe for the crowded, poorly constructed houses.

The deteriorating mansions remained unoccupied for a while, impossible to rent and too expensive to maintain as houses. The buildings might have been destroyed much earlier in the 19th century than they were if streams of immigrants had not begun to arrive at this time. Those who had money usually moved on; but for those who were poor, the North End was the first and only place that they could settle. The Irish advance began sometime after 1824. They settled in the deserted mansions, one family to a room. Germans and English were also there in sufficient number so that one third of the North End population of 20,000 were immigrants of these three nationalities before 1846.[3]

After the disastrous potato famine of 1846, the influx of Irish swelled. Poor, desperate, starving, they began to crowd into the North End and Fort Hill sections of Boston, searching for any means to sustain existence. They took the lowest, meanest jobs in Boston in order to subsist. They came to Boston not because they wanted to live here, but because they could no longer live at home. All through the North End the unfortunate Irish huddled. Overcrowded, undernourished, they were incongruous inhabitants of the once fine houses of the fashionable. The men labored on the railways, worked as street cleaners, factory workers — in any unskilled job that they could obtain. The women hired out as domestics. As foreigners they were alternately tolerated and distrusted, victims of economic conditions over which they had no control. By 1850 they made up one half of the North End population of 23,000. In 1855, 14,000 out of 26,000 North Enders were Irish-born. Many more were probably American-born children of the immigrants. The number of Irish peaked around 1880 and then rapidly dropped off in the face of new immigrant waves.[4] But it was a miserable fifty years that they spent here.

Because so many were illiterate and their chief concern was survival, it is hard to find written records of their life and achievements. Much of what can be gleaned about their life from public records gives

20

only dry statistics about their arrival, diseases, and death. Yet significant things happened. The to-be-famous and the fathers of those who would be famous came out of the indistinguishable mass of human misery. There was achievement — great achievement — when measured against the fact that those who came brought nothing with them to start their new life. Even the scantiest records indicate that backbreaking toil, hope in the power of religion, and a strong sense of political organization were three forces which sustained the Irish through bitter years in the new world. In their reliance on work, God, and the power of government they bear some similarity to the Puritans who had first settled the area. But there were great differences, also, between the Irish who had come unwillingly in despair and desperation and the Puritans who had first come with the purpose of settling a new land. Educated and adventurous, the colonial settlers exercised a degree of choice in their decision to emigrate. In contrast, the threat of starvation which motivated the Irish did not leave them much of an option in their decision to emigrate.

In the 1840's then, the North End became not merely a decaying, older, not-so-fashionable section of town, but one of Boston's first tenement slums. Mansions torn down were replaced by four and five-story tenements. Cheaply made, they served their purpose: to crowd more and more wretched humans into a restricted area. Bostonians, who had never faced this problem before, scarcely knew how to handle it. Their refined senses were shocked by the living conditions of the Irish, conditions they all too often saw, insensitively, as brought on by a shiftless, lazy nature and a low moral standard on the part of the immigrants. However, some philanthropists and moral do-gooders responded to the Irish plight, using the methods of social reform prevalent in that period. In 1839 the Phips mansion became the Asylum for Indigent Boys. Paul Revere's last home had been bought by the Penitent Female Refuge Society in 1824. (It was taken down to build more houses in 1843.)[5] The Boston police, composed mainly of Yankees, regularly got up collections to feed the poor and starving immigrants of the North End.

It is no wonder that disease and a relaxation of accepted moral standards developed in this unhappy situation. Boston had always been a fairly healthy city. There were epidemics, of smallpox mainly, throughout the colonial period, but inoculation and the efforts of the Board of Health had contributed greatly to the control of disease. But by 1845 in Ward 2, which covered the eastern half of the North End, there were 17.79 inhabitants per house. This, when compared to a city-wide average of 10.57, shows how crowded the area was and thus how easily disease could spread.[6] Sickness was abetted by generally unsanitary conditions. Many of the tenements were not connected to sewage systems. Habitations seemed little advanced from medieval days. The result for the poor, inevitably, was death — from cholera,

In the mid-19th century, cheap hotels and boarding houses proliferated in the decaying North Square area.

smallpox, or tuberculosis. In an epidemic of 1849, of 611 deaths in Boston, 114 were in the North End (a large proportion of the rest were in similar Irish areas of Fort Hill). Many of the North End deaths occurred at 136 Hanover Street, a particularly crowded tenement address.[7]

The general squalor contributed to the decline of the North Street (Ann Street) area. One result was the "Beehive," an infamous brothel staffed by many unfortunate girls who possessed no skill to earn a living in any other way. The Beehive itself was emptied in a surprise raid by the enraged citizenry on the night of July 22, 1825. But the "nymphs" of Ann Street existed well into the 1850's. In addition, there was a whole section of low-class boarding houses, gambling dens, dance halls, bistros, and brothels. These provided amusement for sailors and rich boys from uptown who ventured forth on a Saturday night to savor a more exotic life than that offered by sedate Boston society. The rich boys had to be careful lest the evening end earlier for them than they had planned. Sailors and petty thieves were always prepared to divest some unwary boy of his money — and even some of his fancy clothes.

Besides the delights of liquor and women, one could place wagers on such "sports" as rat-baiting. This cruel amusement was especially popular right up through the 1850's. Riots, brawls, muggings, and all manner of crime were so frequent that the district was called the "Black Sea" or the "Murder District." When the navy came in, even the firefighters were called out to stop brawls. Finally, the good citizens of Boston decided that things had gone far enough. A large raid was organized by the police and the night-watchmen (at that time still a separate organization) on the night of April 23, 1851. One hundred and fifty-three people were arrested, including 92 women, most of whom were charged with prostitution. Many of the girls were newcomers and foreigners between the ages of 16 and 30. Undoubtedly, many were Irish girls, victims of a harsh and cruel environment. Known as the "Ann Street Descent," the action marked the beginning of a concerted effort to clean up the area. Ann Street received its present name of North Street. Later (1852) the name was extended to include the stretch of road from Dock Square to North Square, and in 1854 North Street was extended down to Commercial Street. By 1858 the character of the district was improving, but it was still considered "missionary" ground. As late as 1870 even police did not feel safe in the streets unless traveling in groups.[8]

Some of the degradation of Ann Street can be excused in remembering that a sailor's life in the 1900's was extremely rough. After many arduous months at sea, the sailor arrived, his pockets full of money, in a city in which he had no ties of friendship and no home roots. The Rev. E.T. Taylor did much to aid these men through his work in the North End. He established the Seamen's Bethel and the Mariner's House in North Square. There a sailor could relax in a friendly setting, hearing the word of God spoken in a language he could comprehend. The Mariner's House is still a North End landmark, and Rev. Taylor remembered as a sailor's friend.

The attitude of Bostonians toward the Irish immigrants can be illustrated in the career of one North Ender, Bernard "Barney" McGinniskin, Boston's first Irish policeman. McGinniskin was appointed to the force on September 29, 1851, by unanimous vote. When it became known that he was Irish, his appointment was deemed a conflict of interest. Bostonians felt that because so many of the people arrested were Irish, an Irishman would not properly uphold the law against his countrymen. There were already isolated instances of the Irish in public life; however, police duty was considered a position that demanded absolute allegiance to the established order. So meetings were organized in protest to the appointment of McGinniskin, and the police marshall felt obliged to object. (This marshall, a Mr. Tukey, who at the time ran the police like a private organization, had himself acquired money to finance his Harvard education by fleecing sailors on Ann Street in 1848.) McGinniskin reported to work on November 3rd, supposedly shouting out, "Barney McGinniskin from the boys of Ireland!" This was hardly the sort of remark that would endear him to his fellow officers. Marshal Tukey was enraged. In addition to making the "inflammatory" remark, Tukey found McGinniskin guilty of being noisy, quarrelsome, meddlesome (all common insults hurled against the Irish) and claimed that in 1842 he had been involved in a riot in a church. Tukey fired McGinniskin summarily on January 5, 1852. This action brought an outpouring of wrath from local newspapers. The press was of the opinion that the foreign-born should refrain from seeking public positions, but that there was no permissible way to keep them from being appointed if they should be so forward as to apply. McGinniskin was reinstated temporarily but forced out again in 1854.[9] The Know-Nothing Party had by that time spread from New York to Massachusetts. Seeing the Irish as anti-reform, they mounted campaigns against them. Discrimination against the Irish was at its height during their period of power.[10]

The Irish countered the blatant discrimination of the 50's by developing the political organization and enthusiasm that is still very much a factor in Boston politics today. In 1850 Boston was a city of 137,788 people. Half of them were foreign-born, with 53,923 of Irish descent. Only 17,786 foreign-born were registered to vote and only 1,549 voted.[11] Obviously, the foreigners would not get an equal voice in community matters with such a small percentage of the vote. Efforts were made to register people and get them to the polls. Since people were not well educated, opportunistic bosses could easily sway mass opinion and procure a high percentage of the votes cast for themselves or the candidates they represented. Bloc ethnic voting was the result.

The premier politician to come from the Irish North End of this period was John "Honey Fitz" Fitzgerald. Born on Moon Street on February 11, 1863, he gave his first political speech on Hanover Street at the age of 16. Like so many other famous North End boys, he graduated from the Eliot School in 1878. Fitzgerald often ended his speeches with a salute to the "Dear Old North End." At one rally an enthusiastic supporter shouted back a cheer to the "Dearo" and the nickname stuck. Before long there was a political organization known as the Dearos (also as the Jefferson Club), and later the group became merely a social body. Dearos still hold an annual Mass at St. Stephen's or St. Mary's to recall their beginnings in the Dear Old North End. The memorial Mass was begun when Honey Fitz was mayor. Although his daughter Rose Fitzgerald Kennedy was born in the family's home at 4 Garden Court Street in 1890, Fitzgerald later left the North End. He always remembered his North End beginnings with fondness, however, and the people of the North End responded by always giving him their support in his campaigns.

The large Irish community could not be spiritually served by one

Portraits of the North End's Irish political leader John "Honey Fitz" Fitzgerald festoon a North End house.

parish only. In fact, when the Irish first arrived, St. Stephen's was not yet a Catholic church at all. So the Irish formed the first Catholic church in the North End in 1834. Called St. Mary's of the Sacred Heart, it was located on Endicott and Cooper Streets. St. Mary's was only the fifth church in a diocese that at that time covered all of New England. With the large influx of Catholic Irish, the church flourished.

There were disputes in the early history of this church. In 1836 factionalism was so severe between two pastors that the church had to be guarded. A similar disagreement led to a riot in 1842. Conflict was resolved when the Jesuits arrived to staff the church. Jesuits had been banned from preaching in Puritan Boston and the priests of St. Mary's were the first of their order to be allowed to establish a ministry in this city. John McElroy, the first Jesuit pastor of St. Mary's, also became the first president of Boston College in 1863. Many St. Mary's parishioners were among the donors to the college.

The Catholic parishioners were also concerned about the proper education of their children in the Protestant-dominated school system. Therefore, Father McElroy also turned his attention to the establishment of parochial grammar schools. A school for girls had already been formed. In 1849 the Sisters of Notre Dame were invited to come and staff the school, located at that time on Stillman Street. Father Wiget, successor of Father McElroy, founded the Boys School in 1859. For many years it was known popularly as "Father Wiget's School" or simply "The Institute." The school was transferred from site to site in the North End until it reached permanent quarters in 1884 next to the new church, built in 1874 on Cooper Street. The Sisters of Notre Dame, who later staffed Julie Billiart High School as well, were with St. Mary's School throughout the years until it closed in 1973.

St. Mary's Church has played an important role as spiritual and temporal educator throughout its 128-year history. The Irish parishioners are gone now and the congregation has dwindled. There were plans in 1973 and 1974 to replace the church with needed housing for the elderly. Friends of St. Mary's rallied to save the church, and as of mid-1975 they had succeeded, at least temporarily, in stopping the demolition of the North End monument. [12]

While the citizens of Boston were adjusting to their new foreign-born population, events were occurring throughout the country that were to have enormous effects on the future of the whole nation. In the 50's the conflict between the northern and southern states intensified, resulting in the outbreak of the Civil War. This war influenced the treatment of the Irish and other foreign-born citizens. They were needed in the wartime economy to fight and to aid in the manufacture of material and supplies. Economics helped to lessen discrimination.

Many Irish from the North End fought valiantly in the "Fighting Ninth," the Ninth Regiment of Massachusetts Volunteers. Their leader was the Irish-born and American-raised Colonel Thomas Cass who lived at 14 North Bennet Street. Colonel Cass was killed in battle on July 12, 1862, and his body brought home for burial. The funeral services were noteworthy for their magnificence and for the great crowds that were attracted. It was the largest funeral procession Boston had seen until that time. The response to Cass's death was an indication of the involvement felt by North Enders in the Civil War struggle. On the whole, they supported the war effort strongly.

However, the practice of conscription in the Civil War led to the first draft riots in this country. Rich men conscripted could buy their way out of army duty or send a substitute. As usual, the poor had no choice — they had to serve! Angered, protesters surfaced in New York and Boston. On July 14, 1863, officers who were attempting to serve notices of conscription on Prince Street were beaten by a mob of North Enders. The mob, encouraged by its success, moved on to attack a gunhouse on Cooper Street. Their object was cannon stored in the building. In the ensuing melee several people in the garrison and at least eight rioters were killed. The following day the mob returned, but this time they were quieted by the rector of St. Mary's church. Further tragedy was averted. [13]

The Irish population in the North End continued to increase until about 1880. At that time Copp's Hill was familiarly referred to as "Connemara Hill" because of the numbers of Galway men resident there, and Donegal men settled around "Donegal Square." However, the Irish immigration slowed in later years and the old families began to move out of the slum district as they acquired the wealth to do so. But before the so-called "second wave" of immigration that descended on the North End in the 80's and 90's, some forerunners of the thousands to come were already settling in the midst of the Irish.

Marquis Niccolo Reggio has been called the first Italian to settle in Boston. [14] Born of a Genoese family, he arrived in 1832. While in Boston, he served as consul for the Papal States, Sardinia and the Two Sicilies. His daughter Rosa taught school in the North End for 50 years. She was the principal of the Pormont School located in Snelling Place off Hull Street. Marquis Reggio was typical of the foreigner who settled in Boston in the earliest years of the 19th century. There was always a sprinkling of French, Italians, and Germans who, usually well-educated, handled consular affairs, conducted music or dance lessons, or engaged in some other business to which their backgrounds made them especially well-suited. This small group of foreigners was apt to be easily accepted by society. Few in number, they posed no threat to the accepted order. Precisely because of their exotic background, they were considered exciting additions to society. They were not at all representative of the vast numbers of later immigrants.

By the 1860's the first definite Italian settlement was taking shape.

It was composed mainly of Genoese. Like Reggio, even the poor in this group of northern Italians were better educated and brought more money with them than the southerners who followed. This Italian immigrant group settled on Ferry Court off North Street. At this time North Street was still a very rundown area, an area where cheap housing would be available to a newly arriving group. The Genoese gradually extended the area of their settlement along Ferry Street and North Street, moving by the 1880's along North Street down to Cross Street at one end and North Bennet Street at the other. A colony of Sicilians, Genoese, and a sprinkling of other Italians were heavily concentrated on North Bennet Street. As the Italian community spread from its small nucleus on Ferry Court, the Irish retreated.

The early Genoese assimilated reasonably well into the society around them. Of course, they were a very small group. In 1880 there were still only 1,277 Italians in all of Boston. However, as their numbers grew, tension developed between the Italians and the Irish. Many of the Irish, now second generation, looked down on the arriving Italians in much the same way as they had been looked down upon by the native-born Yankees. They perceived the Italians to be an economic threat. Like all immigrant groups, the Italians were grateful to be allowed to work long hours for extremely low wages. The Irish feared competition for the menial jobs which they had held unchallenged. Economic fear was augmented by a general misunderstanding of each other's customs. For the Irish, street-fighting and gang battles were sports. For the Italians, this was serious provocation. They retaliated, not with fists, but with knives. This, in turn, was completely unheard of in Irish society. Soon the two groups were keeping well apart. The lone Italian or Irishman venturing out of his territory was likely to be attacked. Since the Irish vastly outnumbered the Italians of the early settlement, members of the Italian community left Ferry Court in the morning for work, returned in the evening, and rarely ventured out at night. [15]

The areas settled by the new arrivals were the least accessible to waterfront or commercial activities. The Irish, though dwindling, still inhabited choice property on Commercial Street as late as 1911. The newest arrival got the least desirable dwelling. The Italians settled together for safety and the reassurance of being with other immigrants of their nationality. Therefore, they had little choice in their housing.

The Italians were not the only arrivals. A small Portuguese colony sprang up, located mainly on Fleet Street. Most of the Portuguese were fishermen, and major Portuguese settlements developed not in the North End, but in Gloucester and New Bedford. However, there were enough Portuguese residents to form their own church, Saint John the Baptist, near the corner of North Bennet and Hanover Street. [16] This church served the colony into the 20th century when it was acquired by the city for use as a library.

Chapter Three
THE "NEW WAVE"
OF IMMIGRATION
1880 to 1920

1880 was a critical year in the development of the North End. Once again outside forces combined to change the character of this community. Just as the Irish potato famine of 1846 had provided the impetus for the earlier flood of immigrants, so conditions in southern and eastern Europe unleashed an unprecedented waved of immigrants upon the eastern seaboard. The Jews faced oppression because of their religion. Pogroms threatened their lives if they stayed in Russia, Poland, and other eastern European countries. The southern Italian was beset by an oppressive rise in taxes (taking as much as 54% of a family's income) coupled with natural disasters that led to increasingly poor crops in years when the population was burgeoning. Inadvertently, the unification of Italy became a disaster for the south. Old traditions of enmity between south and north were exacerbated because the south could not contribute its share economically in a united Italy. Hundreds of years of corruption and decadence had bled the land dry. Thus, like the Irish before them, the destitute, the starving, the persecuted, the uneducated, the unskilled began packing their meager belongings to make the trip from Italy to America and a new opportunity. Unfortunately, since they arrived penniless and friendless, their dream soon gave way to the realities of life in a coastal city slum — long hours of work at low pay to keep from utter starvation.[1]

Population figures show dramatically how the tide swung in the North End. In 1855, 14,000 out of 26,000 North Enders were Irish. In 1880 the Irish had increased and there were little more than 1,000 Italians in the North End. By 1895, however, there were 7,700 Italians, 800 Portuguese, 6,200 Jews, 1,200 British, and only 6,800 Irish.[2] The Irish population declined swiftly after that.

As the Irish left, the Jewish community arrived, and the Italian community continued its expansion. Today only a few names on stores along Salem Street remain to remind the passer-by that at one time this street was the center of a thriving Jewish community which formed nearly one third of the North End's population around 1895. As the Genoese had all settled together — partly for protection, partly because no other housing was available, partly because of a natural gravitation toward their own kind — so the arriving Jews preferred settling with their friends and relatives who had recently come over. As new immigrants arrived, often possessing little more than the clothes they wore, they would move in with earlier arrivals until a job or other lodging could be found. As an area became filled with one ethnic group, another would retreat before it. Houses surrounding the group would become available and the community would grow out from its center.

The Jewish immigrants settled in a triangular area nearly one-quarter mile on each side, extending roughly from Hanover Street to Endicott Street and back to Prince Street. Salem, Cross, Stillman, North Margin, and Parmenter Streets, Baldwin, Salem, Noyes, and Bartlett Place were included. There were other earlier Jewish settlements in Boston, but they were composed mainly of German Jews. The Russian and other eastern Jews felt no closer a bond with their German co-religionists than southern and northern Italians felt for each other. Regarded as outsiders by the more westernized German Jew, they formed a separate settlement in the North End. The first Jewish residents were arriving in the 70's, just as the first sprinkling of Genoese had arrived before the great wave of the 80's. By 1873 there were sufficient numbers to found a congregation, Congregation Beth Abraham. In 1890 Congregation Beth Israel was formed on Baldwin Place.

The foundations of Jewish life in the North End were family, religion, and business. A strong family life was always important to the Jewish community. At first its development was hampered, as it was for the Italians and other immigrant groups, by the large proportion of men among the first immigrants. A father, brother, or fiance would be sent over to earn the money necessary either to ease poverty at home or bring the rest of the family over. When the family arrived, sometimes after years of separation, the heavy demands made upon the father's time by the necessity of working long hours made him often absent from his home. Much of the child's upbringing depended on the mother in these circumstances. Proper education, both religious and secular, was considered extremely important and definitely engaged a father's interest. Early families employed a private "rebbe" to come in and give religious instruction, especially that necessary for the Bar Mitzvah. Public education was also encouraged. The Eliot School in 1906 was two-thirds Jewish and a proper education was seen as essential for social integration and economic advancement. Girls attended the Hancock School. Few at this time could afford to send their children on to higher education, but traditions of scholarship and study were not forgotten, merely preceded by the more pressing concerns of making a good living.

While providing a location for the religious education of the young and for religious services, the synagogues were also a gathering point for the whole community, expecially the male members. The Russian Jews were devoutly orthodox. As late as 1903 there was nearly a riot when a store opened on the Sabbath Day. In later years the sons and daughters of the immigrants did not observe orthodox rules as strictly. Even some anti-religionists and socialists appeared in the community. As elsewhere, this ethnic community saw a split develop between the original immigrants and members of the new generation, whose assimilation into the new culture resulted in their rejecting some of the more restrictive traditions of the past.

The majority of the Jewish immigrants had a village or small town background and were not peasants or farmers as the earlier Irish and the southern Italians were. They brought with them a traditional respect for scholarship and learning and an orientation to business. They proved themselves well suited to the task of starting over in a new land. One of the first trades undertaken by many of the Jewish immigrants was that of peddler. With only a small outlay of cash, a man could buy enough goods to make a journey of a few days or a week and turn sufficient profit to support himself. The peddler sold linens, kitchen utensils, knickknacks, and occasionally even groceries house to house. By dint of hard work, he might eventually advance himself sufficiently to begin supplying other peddlers as did eight former peddlers in forming Harris Gorfinkle and Company in 1888, or Freedman Brothers. Other families became clothing retailers — Richmond, Cohen and Reinherz, and Michael Slutsky. Soon there were small businesses of all kinds — real estate, tailoring, money-lending — that prospered and grew through the immigrants' efforts. Even women were encouraged to help. Yente Rabinowitz opened a small grocery store. Bernard Berenson, world famous art critic, grew up watching his mother run a small luncheonette.

The community in general prospered and many famous people began their careers in the North End. Sophie Tucker, while living at 22 Salem Street, attended the Cushman School and made her first appearance as an actress at the Howard Athenaeum in Boston. The Cushman School on Parmenter Street stood on the site of the birthplace of another famous actress, Charlotte Cushman, also a North Ender. The Stop and Shop food chain grew out of a store owned by the Rabinowitz family. Bankers (such as Albert Ginzberg and I. Reinherz), religious leaders of the stature of Rabbi Margolies (later head of the New York congregation), and doctors (including heart specialist Dr. Samuel Levine) — all were products of this small ethnic community in a slum area of Boston. Success had its price. As the second generation grew and prospered, they moved out of the neighborhood and assimilated into the larger community. By 1910 the last North End Jews were moving on into the mainstream of society, leaving the North End and its memories of poverty behind them. [3]

The southern Italian immigrants who began arriving in the 1880's were reluctant to make the transition to a new way of life. At first there was some doubt about whether and how long they would stay. As late as 1901, 79% of the Italian immigrants to America were men, known

Old North Church near the end of the 19th century as seen from Hull Street.

as "birds of passage" because so many did not settle, but moved back and forth from Italy to the United States.[4] Yet the sheer numbers who arrived were so great that they had a staggering effect on the city of Boston. As noted above, there were 7,700 Italians in the North End in 1895. This had been a large increase compared to the 1,000 residents fifteen years earlier. Within the next 20 years the number of foreign-born in Boston increased 763%. In 1895, 1.5% of the Boston population was Italian. In 1920, 15.7% was Italian. The large majority of these immigrants were male and of working age.

More than any other area in Boston, the North End underwent a spectacular increase in Italian population. 26.6% of the North End was Italian in 1895.[5] In 1920, 90% of the population was of Italian stock. The absolute numbers of the population also rose dramatically. In this small enclave of the city the 1895 population was 23,000. In 1900 it was 28,000. By 1920, 40,000 people lived in the district. The North End, always a crowded, congested section of the city was bursting at the seams. Only Calcutta could boast more people per square mile![6] Comparison with the North End today gives these statistics added impact. The North End still has a high population density, visible in the crowded streets and densely packed houses. Yet the population is barely one-third of the population of 1920!

The results of this severe overcrowding were not surprising. Even in 1891, 154 families in the North End were living in one room per family! In both Boston and New York the death rate for children under five skyrocketed. The North End had become Boston's "classic land of poverty."[7] By 1920 the tenement houses in which the immigrants lived were already 50 to 60 years old. (99.6% of the houses were built before 1919.) All were three-to-five story walk-up apartments without private baths or central heating. 74.5% of the families shared toilets, 13.6% shared water.[8] As the Italians realized that their future lay in remaining in America, they sought to buy and eventually upgrade property. Owning real estate was important to these former peasants whose culture had taught them to value land. In 1902, 19.08% of the real estate was owned by Italian residents. In 1922, 50.70%. One of the first things a family saved for was its own property, often undertaking great sacrifices and foregoing other material comforts.[9]

Who were these newest arrivals in America? Like the Irish, they were mainly peasants from small hamlets and villages. As noted before, males and working-age people predominated in the early years. They were largely uneducated and had an extremely high illiteracy rate. Only 10 of 15,616 southern Italians arriving in 1903 could read. 49.1% were totally illiterate in 1900. At least half of those arriving spoke no English. They were desperately poor. In 1901 Frederick Bushee estimated that the average southern Italian brought only $9.00 with him to Boston. The new arrival depended on obtaining lodging with his relatives or *paesani* (Italians of the same village or area) for survival. It was not unusual for 10 or 12 men to share one room. Nearly 30% of the households contained one or more boarders.[10]

Survival meant finding a job — any job — and working the long hours needed to get a substantial wage. The potential worker who spoke no English was often dependent upon a padrone. The padrone would arrange a job but in return would take a healthy percentage of the unfortunate worker's salary as a commission. Some padrones were fair in their assessments, but others took advantage of their countrymen's ignorance to increase their own wealth. As 64.5% of the men were unskilled laborers, the jobs open to them were limited. Some found work in the many North End factories. A few went into the shoemaking business. Others worked on the docks. Italian fishermen, mainly Sicilians, clustered around "T" Wharf. Work was found in granite and stone quarries or as brick masons. Construction laborers left Boston daily or for the week to build the Brockton and Beverly sewers, the Northampton reservoir, or to work on railways. Over 50% of the men were engaged in freight handling, construction, or railroad work. Only 1.4% of the

Small fruit and vegetable shops, founded by immigrants, flourish today in the North End's market area.

population worked at jobs that could be classified as professional and 1.5% were clerks. [11]

A few set up small businesses in fruit and produce. Many of these developed from pushcarts peddling produce in the market district. Older residents can remember pushcarts lined up on a Saturday morning to race for the most advantageous position in the market. Italian ethnic foods, exotic to American tastes, were marketed first for the Italian population and then to the general public. The first macaroni sold in Boston was a non-Italian egg macaroni produced on Commercial Street in 1874. John Ponte may have been the first manufacturer of Italian macaroni in 1881. He became head of the Boston Macaroni Company in 1890. The Prince Macaroni Company, famous in New England, was founded by Michael LaMarca, Joseph Scaminara, and Michael Cantella. The Maravigna Macaroni Company, begun on Fleet Street in 1913, produced an award-winning product. That all-time favorite, pizza, was introduced to the Boston public in 1908 in Guiseppe Parziale's shop at 78 Prince Street. [12] Slowly, through all these occupations, the Italians sought to improve their low economic status.

Not only men, but women were forced to work to support the family. The women were even less likely than the men to venture out from the North End. Almost all the women worked at local factories with other North End Italian-speaking employees. It was extremely rare for an Italian woman to seek work as a domestic as so many of the young Irish had done. The women may have been allowed to work, but they were still protected and sheltered within their community structure. The women received even less compensation for their labors than men did. A typical female worker in a garment factory made from $3.00 to $5.00 weekly. Men at the same job earned approximately $9.00. [13] These low wages were paid for weeks that frequently averaged 60 hours: 10 hours a day, six days a week. Such arduous working conditions seem unbearable to today's observer, yet they were not unusual at the time. For those who had emigrated because of necessity, even these dismal jobs and surroundings represented opportunity.

Popular opinion expressed in magazine articles of the day pictured the immigrant, especially the Italian, as shiftless, lazy and unwilling to work steadily. As workers, Italians were not supposed to be as strong or dependable as the Irish, but given to moodiness and always eager to lay down work for play. The inaccuracy of such stereotypes is evidenced in the long hours they worked, the primitive conditions in which they lived, and the fact that, arriving with no wealth, they quickly scrimped and saved to bring over families, to buy houses, or to open businesses.

One characteristic that had marked the Irish community of the North End was their skill at political organization and their strength at the voting booth. The Italian immigrants,coming mainly from the south of Italy, had learned through centuries of conquest and oppression to distrust all government. They were extremely apathetic about obtaining their citizenship and did not really believe that their united voice could be effectively used at the polls to better their lives. In 1868 only twelve Italian-surnamed people voted in Boston. All were from the North End, several on North Street and several on Stillman Street. City records of 1871 show the names of 40 males over 21 with none registered to vote. In 1909 only 20.8% of the Italian population surveyed had American citizenship. Thus the Italians never controlled their own ward. In 1871 this was Ward 2. Irish political figures, representing a minority of the population, were elected every time. By 1915, when it looked as if Italian voters were beginning to gain political control, the North End was combined with West and South End wards. The political machine of Martin Lomasney helped keep Italians out of local politics for nearly another 20 years. [14]

Tension between the arriving Italians and the resident Irish in the North End has already been mentioned. Different customs, attitudes, and manner of living kept the two groups antagonistic. Even though they shared a common bond of religion — Catholicism — in a Protestant environment, their different backgrounds led naturally to the desire to establish separate churches. St. Leonard's, founded in 1873, is not only the oldest Italian church in the North End, but the second oldest in the United States. [15] It was organized and staffed by Franciscans under the leadership of Father Joachim Guerini. Besides Sunday religious services, the Italian church sponsored weekly devotions to St. Anthony and encouraged religious and social clubs similar to parish life as the immigrants had known it in their own homeland. Another religious-social aid society was responsible for the foundation of Sacred Heart Church. St. Mark's Society was formed by the early Genoese settlers after the Civil War. In 1888 they purchased the Protestant church known as Father Taylor's Bethel on the corner of North Square. The Missionary Fathers of St. Charles Borromeo came to staff the church and have remained as spiritual leaders through the intervening years. [16]

Education for the children was also a concern of the Italian families of the parish. In 1903 St. John's School was opened under the auspices of the Missionary Sisters of the Sacred Heart. In 1912 the school was added to the parish of the Sacred Heart Church and the Sisters of St. Joseph took over teaching duties. In the 1920's St. Leonard's Church sponsored St. Anthony's School, the North End's third parochial grammar school.

Although not politically motivated, the Italian immigrants were social people and they believed in helping each other. Soon after arrival, the *paesani* established social clubs and mutual aid groups, thus maintaining their associations from the old country. One of the customary duties of these societies was to honor their patron saint with a yearly religious festival. It is hard to determine exactly when the *feste* began, but they were definitely organized by the first decade of the 20th century. The Feast of Our Lady of Grace, sponsored by former villagers of San Sossio Baronia, has been celebrated since 1903. The Sicilian fishermen instituted a festival in honor of La Madonna del Soccorso in 1910. [17] Each year the fleet would gather in the harbor to be blessed. Celebrations would thank the Madonna for her help in safeguarding the fishermen while at sea. The procession of a statue of the saint around the North End was always part of the festival.

Other societies honored Saint Anthony, Saint Rocco, and other patron saints. Saint Agrippina di Mineo was honored by a society that originally was composed solely of men from the town of Mineo. Festivals continue today all through the summer weekends, preserving old customs in a blend of piety and gala reunion. The *feste* inspire Italians now living elsewhere to return to the North End and see old faces. They have developed into one of the most well-known North End traditions expressing for many the essence of the Italian character of the district.

The Paul Revere House before restoration early in the 20th century.

The immigrants also honored a secular hero, Christopher Columbus. The Genoese formed the Societa Italiana Cristoforo Colombo in 1859. It was incorporated as a benevolent society in 1869. By 1890, through the efforts of this group, a memorial to Columbus was planned. At its unveiling in 1892 there was a grand celebration marking the 400th anniversary of Columbus' discovery. This was the first Columbus Day. Italian-Americans spearheaded the drive to make the holiday a permanent one. Finally in 1910 a bill was passed by the Massachusetts General Court making Columbus Day an official holiday.[18]

As the Italian population established a numerical majority, the streets of the North End, still considered a land of abject misery and poverty, took on the characteristics of an Italian town. The people spent as much time as possible outside, gathered on street corners or in parks. The traditional Italian interest in gambling was continued, but otherwise crime was low in the disrict. In the culture from which the people came, gambling was not considered illegal, but a legitimate amusement. Although early discriminatory writers had feared the growth of immigrant crime, this fear was largely unfounded and the instances of serious crime were few. Likewise, alcoholism was an evil feared by the dominant society which never materialized into a serious problem in the immigrant community.

The Italian immigrant's strong social and family organization helped him adjust to a land where life was different in many ways. He had exchanged the countryside for the city, a warm climate for a cold one. There was a new language, new food, a difference in government and education. New skills were needed to achieve economic advancement in the society. Then there were also the lingering effects of discrimination to be faced. However, the immigrant could not solve all his problems solely through self-help and friendship organizations. Outside agencies came into existence to aid the immigrant as philanthropically-minded Bostonians became aware of the potential problems of settling the flood of immigrants.

One of the thoughtful, generous people was Pauline Agassiz Shaw. As a member of the Boston Association of Charities, she became aware of the social and adjustment problems that had arisen in the North End. In 1884, through her efforts, the Boston Association of Charities secured a building on the corner of North Bennet and Salem Streets. Originally the Salem Street Congregational Church, it had become the home of the Boston Seaman's Friend's Society in 1872. Called at first the North End Industrial Home, it was envisioned as an experiment in social work in which "not alms but a friend, not gifts but employment" would be extended to the immigrants. The ideal sought by the Industrial Home was the achievement of social betterment through education. First efforts were therefore in the area of manual training and improvement. This training was extended to school boys from the Eliot in September 1883 and by 1885, 300 boys and girls were employed. The program was so successful that in 1885 a corporation was formed to purchase the property and the North Bennet Street Industrial School was launched. It was the first organization of its kind in America and, in keeping with its historic position, has pioneered in so many educational areas that it is impossible to list all its contributions. In 1885 classes for cooking for girls at the Hancock School were begun. These were later assumed by the Boston school system and were the first public school kitchens in America. The first public kindergarten and nursery began here as well.

In 1888 Sloyd, a Swedish method of manual training, was introduced into this country for the first time at North Bennet Industrial School. Mr. Gustaf Larsson taught not only local boys, but trained other teachers in this technique from his workshops on North Bennet Street. Prevocational classes to integrate school experience with work experience were begun with boys from the Eliot and girls from the Hancock School. The students received valuable experience in printing, woodworking, sheet metal, and electric wiring, or sewing, cooking, and designing. The Paul Revere lunchroom was built by the boys and staffed by the girls. Daily the young women served lunches, assuming all the responsibility for budget, preparation and serving of the meal. This practical experience was combined with their school lessons so that students could appreciate the concrete results of their formal education. A civic service center was founded in 1901, and the first vocational guidance bureau in the country was also begun there. The guidance bureau was so successful that again the Boston schools became interested in the program. A travel camp was begun in 1903 to enable city children to escape from the confines of urban life and enjoy fresh air in the countryside. Settlement house programs provided boys' and girls' clubs, scouting, a gym and recreational facilities for adults. The Boy Scout troop, established in 1916, was one of the first urban troops in the country.

The travel camp provided opportunities for some North End youngsters to leave the heat of the city, but only for brief periods. Norman A. Franzeim, who had become affiliated with North Bennet Street Industrial School in 1915 as director of Shaw House (the settlement house) felt that the establishment of caddy camps would provide a greater opportunity for the boys. One of the first such camps, Maplewood Caddy Camp, established in 1915, made it possible for a young boy to spend the whole summer in a healthy atmosphere, pay his expenses, and perhaps even earn some extra money to bring home. The boys were taught the responsibility of work and encouraged to help each other in camp. The caddy camp tradition has continued to the present, although Mr. Franzeim retired in 1949. Maplewood was closed in 1964, and a second camp in Bethlehem has also been closed, but the program still operates on Cape Cod.

As if the catalogue of "firsts" were not long enough already, North Bennet Street was also the site of the first credit union organized in a settlement house. Joseph Campana, known as the "father of credit unions," helped organize the union which opened on September 1, 1921, with capital of $14.25. When the charter was granted, there were but 11 members. Two months later there were 33 with a combined savings of $1,486. Two years later 243 members had contributed assets of $5,099. Even children were encouraged to contribute their dimes and pennies. Loans were given to local people that no other bank would approve because the North End at that time was considered a high-risk slum area. Yet the people worked hard and they used their loans to build businesses, repair homes, and upgrade their neighborhood. The Social Service Credit Union helped make much of this possible.

The North End Union was established in 1892 by the Benevolent Fraternity of Unitarian Churches. It also boasts many firsts in its long history of service to the people of the North End. The predecessor of the Union, The Children's Mission, organized the first supervised playground in the country in 1886. The education of young men in useful skills was an early concern. To further this aim, the Union sponsored the first school of plumbing in New England in 1894 and the first printing school in 1900. Both of these enterprises were eventually taken over by Wentworth Institute. Health care was provided by a milk station opened in 1893; the public baths began in 1894; the summer camp in 1904; a dental dispensary in cooperation with Tufts Dental School in 1907; and a pre-natal and well-baby clinic in 1918. All health activities were transferred to the White Health Fund Unit no. 1 when it opened on North Margin street in 1924. North Enders also benefitted from the Fruit and Flower Mission. Fresh flowers and produce collected from suburban gardens were distributed by the Union on Thursdays, brightening the day of many North End youngsters and their families. Citizenship and health classes, begun in 1895, continued until 1955. Besides classes and health programs, the Union was also a full-scale settlement house offering a wide range of recreational activities, arts and crafts, and summer outing programs. This aspect resulted in the foundation of Camp Parker in Pembroke, Massachusetts in 1923. In the 83 years of its service thousands of North End residents have benefitted from the many opportunities available in the Union. In recent years the Union has expanded to make room for various city and government programs. Today the Little City Hall is located in the building along with a complete range of counseling services. [19]

The Boston Public Library has also had a long history of service to North End families. Service began in 1882 with a book delivery station in the Hancock School building on Parmenter Street. In 1890 the operation moved to 166 Hanover Street and continued for six years until temporarily removed to the West End. On June 1, 1899, the delivery station was reopened in the North Bennet Street Industrial School. The immigrant children were early and enthusiastic users of the facility. They seemed to have a hunger for books that delighted library staff. The response proved so overwhelming that the North End Branch moved to its own building at 3A North Bennet Street, formerly the church of Saint John the Baptist, in 1912. At that time the library had a collection that included not only English but Italian and Yiddish books, reflecting the ethnic composition of its neighborhood. This responsiveness to neighborhood needs has resulted in the maintenance of its Italian literature collection. Reading groups and book clubs sponsored by the library were popular and well attended. [20]

The most successful library group was the Saturday Evening Girls. These young working girls were brough together by librarian Edith Guerrier in 1899 when the library was in the Industrial School. As part of their activities, the girls began to contribute an hour a week to common projects, including the Paul Revere Pottery Workshop in 1908. The name for the pottery developed naturally from its location in the historic North End. Mrs. James Storrow, wife of a prominent Boston banker, bought a house and converted it for the girls' use in 1912. The pottery succeeded and soon became a full-scale business for the girls who, unlike their neighbors, worked in clean bright surroundings in a comfortable building. The pottery was sold nationally and even Queen Mary of England ordered a set. By 1915 the business had expanded sufficiently to move to larger quarters in Brighton. The girls earned as much as $10 a week, a good salary at that time, and received the additional bonus of working in pleasant conditions. In 1975 an exhibition of the pottery was mounted to coincide with Bicentennial activities. Pieces of pottery from this small North End enterprise are now valuable antiques treasured by collectors.

Other community services were instituted to aid the immigrants. The Hull Street Medical Mission was founded in 1894 by the Woman's Division of Christian Services of the Methodist Church. Medical care was dispensed to the needy by them and also by the George White Health Unit which took over services offered by the North End Union. Both ceased service in 1961. Today health care is given by the North End Community Health Center on Hanover Street. The Boston Baptist Bethel and Mariner's House attended to the physical and spiritual needs of sailors who were still prominent figures on North End streets. The Post Office was another popular savings institute. They received 4,000,000 dollars from their frugal Italian customers, the second highest total for any post office in the United States. [21]

North Enders were very thrifty. This belief in saving has been demonstrated by the success of the Credit Union and the large deposits in the Post Office. Unfortunately, they — along with countless other

Bostonians — were "taken in" by one bad investment. Many North Enders lost money in the swindles of Charles Ponzi whose confidence scheme was the sensation of the day when it was uncovered. Ponzi, an Italian immigrant, turned a borrowed $200 into a $15-million fortune while thousands of hard-working citizens lost their savings. Idolized throughout the 20's and 30's before his schemes were uncovered, he met justice at last and was deported in 1937.

Chapter Four
AN ETHNIC COMMUNITY
1920 until the Present Day

World War I resulted in the temporary cessation of immigration to America. By this time the Italians held a clear numerical majority in the North End. Indeed, by 1920 the district was over 90% Italian. The inhabitants of the North End had come to regard this area as their home. Dreams of going back to Italy remained for many, but the majority had realized long since that their future was in this country. As friends and relatives joined the early arrivals, ties with Italy — though always strong — became a little less compelling. The family was here.

When World War I broke out, Italians served their adopted country in various branches of the armed forces. The first man drafted in World War I was a North Ender. Joseph Cefalo lived at 5 Hull Street, opposite the Old North Church. When number 258 was pulled from the bowl of draft numbers, Joseph Cefalo was the person designated to be drafted. When the war had run its course and Joseph Cefalo and all his comrades had done their soldiering, another scourge struck the North End.[1] In 1918 the world-wide epidemic of the flu decimated the people of the North End.

During the first part of the 20th century the North End remained an area of industrial activity in addition to serving an enormous residential population. A prominent landmark was the molasses tank on Commercial Street. On January 15, 1919, at 12:30 p.m. the tank suddenly split, engulfing the surrounding street in a tidal wave of sticky, suffocating molasses. The wave formed by this monstrous flood was 15 feet high. Nearly 2.2 million gallons exploded from the four-year-old tank. Twenty-one people were killed and more than 100 were hospitalized in the ensuing catastrophe. The dead included teamsters and school children, city workers and innocent passers-by. Buildings were demolished; a firehouse and several houses collapsed under the relentless pressure of the gooey substance which swept all before it. It took 500 men over a week of round-the-clock work to clear the streets of molasses and wreckage. Even fireboats were pressed into service to spray down the area. A few older residents can still remember the tragedy in which some of their classmates died. It is often said that, over 55 years later, a faint odor of molasses can be detected on a summer day.

As residents came to realize that they would always live in the United States, they began to think of the North End as their neighborhood. To outsiders it was still a slum, however — an eyesore and a

Eventually immigrants in the North End bought homes and raised families there, signifying their commitment to life in a new land.

blight on the image of Boston. The first threats of urban renewal and development began in 1919. The City Planning Board proposed the creation of "Lafayette Street" to connect the North End and Charlestown across the Charlestown Bridge. This plan would have effectively split the North End in half. The Italian citizens, never before a strong political force, erupted in unified protest and the plan was abandoned.[2]

In 1920 the North End was back in the national spotlight as attention focused on Nicola Sacco and Bartolomeo Vanzetti. After World War I, the United States was gripped by a "Red scare." All persons suspected of radical or Bolshevik viewpoints were the target of public opprobrium. A number of Massachusetts — including North End — Italians professed anarchistic philosophies and were therefore branded as anti-American. This general unrest little aided the Italians as a group in combatting discrimination, but instead heightened latent fears about their motives in immigrating and their trustworthiness as citizens. At the height of this anti-radical scare, the paymaster and guard of a shoe factory were killed and robbed of $16,000 in South Braintree on April 15, 1920. Sacco and Vanzetti, both immigrants and professed anarchists, were arrested shortly, tried and convicted of the crime. Public opinion at home was unanimous in demanding their execution; throughout the world, however, famous intellectuals examined the evidence and declared the trial hopelessly prejudiced against the defendants because of their origins and beliefs. Sacco and Vanzetti maintained their innocence steadfastly, but although many critics believed that sound proof of their guilt was lacking, all attempts to save them failed. They were executed on August 23, 1927. Their guilt is still widely disputed nearly fifty years later. Many of the Italian-American residents of the North End regard their death as one of the more extreme instances of discriminatory actions against people of Italian descent. At their wake and funeral in the North End, thousands of people, some simply curious, but many more dismayed or angered, came to view the bodies.

As the community grew, it developed a need for self-expression. This need was answered by the *Italian News*, first issued on February 19, 1921. The *News* related items of interest to Italian-Americans, drawing on local events and items of national and international importance that were of special interest to this group. The paper was an important document of North End events throughout its history.

In the late twenties Italian-Irish rivalry moved into a new arena. The traditional dislike had continued after the Irish had left the North End. Fights across the Charlestown Bridge were as frequent a fact of life for the young men and boys throughout the 30's and 40's as they had been a diverting colonial sport. However, with the rise of prohibition, competition for control of the liquor industry grew more intense. The boss of these illicit operations in the 20's and 30's was Jewish. By 1930 there were two powerful gangs, one operating from the North End and one from South Boston, vying for control of this lucrative business.[3] Gang warfare was an inevitable and unfortunate result of this illegal activity. While organized crime had existed in this country before Italian immigration to America, it was at this time that it became identified solely with persons of Italian descent. The American fascination with the gangster image has contributed to the durability of the association that persists in identifying Italians as potential gangsters and the North End as a center of organized crime.

Around this period, also, the North End witnessed a curious reversal of its usual population flow. Encouraged by the ambience of the area and the low rents, several artists moved into the North End, the first time that non-immigrants had consciously chosen to live there in more than 100 years. Robert S. Chase, portrait painter and decorator, was one of the first of these new Bohemians to make the move.[4] He left studios on Beacon Hill to restore a beautiful old house on Snowhill Street. Later he designed the bronzes in the Paul Revere Mall.

The thirties were a relatively quiet time for North Enders. The general result of the depression on the country was also felt here. Work was hard to find. More men were free to spend their days on the street corner or in local clubs. The population of the North End peaked in the 20's and by 1930 was decreasing. It had already gone from a high of about 36,000 in 1920 to just a little over 21,000 ten years later. It would continue to decrease. As with other immigrant groups, members of the second generation were being assimilated into the mainstream of American life. As sons and daughters grew up, attended school, married and got better jobs, they left the crowded North End for suburban communities. East Boston, Revere, Somerville, Everett, Medford, Quincy, Braintree — in communities throughout the North and South Shores, Italian families settled. Of the North End's population, 59.46% was composed of second-generation Italians, yet they accounted for 76.42% of the emigration.[5] It seemed apparent that the North End Italians would go the way of early migrations. Soon only the old and the unsuccessful would be left behind. Perhaps they would be swallowed up by a new immigrant group; perhaps with the increasing pressure of commercial development the North End would become totally devoid of a resident population. However, immigration never ceased. As long as conditions in Italy remained sufficiently bad, there would always be candidates eager to begin a new life in America. Also those that left the North End maintained close ties with the area. Parents and friends, remaining behind, brought departing North Enders back to the area often. Some successful North Enders stayed out of choice. The North End was their home and they had an affection for it. They were among long-time friends and they enjoyed the Italian atmosphere of the community. There were conflicts between generations and even conflicts between different groups in the North End, but an essential unity remained. The sociological classic, *Street Corner Society* is a comprehensive examination of the community in this period. While it does not detail events (all names are disguised), it tries to render the flavor of life at this time.

In 1930 the Catholic Charitable Bureau, under the administration of the Sisters of St. Joseph, founded the Catherine Moore House to function as a settlement house offering crafts and classes. As the second generation grew up, there was not as great a need for basic educational and vocational skills, although the need did not vanish entirely. However, recreational and social activities remained important in this crowded and still somewhat poor district.

The need for open space was recognized by Boston's Mayor Curley in authorizing the building of the Prado or, as it is officially known, Paul Revere Mall. Several narrow tenement streets were cleared out and the mall established in 1933.[6] The Prado was an instant success with local residents. It provided a natural gathering place for men and women to meet for conversation or card playing and for neighborhood children to play. Since the mall connected Old North Church on Salem Street and St. Stephen's on the opposite side of Hanover Street, it seemed a logical place for the erection of plaques recalling some of the historical events that had occurred in the North End. These are the plaques designed by Robert Savage Chase, then a

46

Continuing the traditions of the old country, Italian men enjoy an afternoon socializing in the Prado.

resident of Snowhill Street. The plaques remind visitors not only of well-known events, but also of other minor but equally interesting occurrences. The land that the Prado stands on was originally part of a pasture belonging to Christopher Stanley. As noted before, he bequeathed some of his land for the establishment of a free school, thus becoming the first private benefactor of public education. Samuel Francis Smith, the author of "America" ("My Country Tis of Thee") lived for a while on Sheafe Street. John Winthrop, Nicholas Upsall, Ann Pollard — names familiar and unfamiliar are preserved there.

What more appropriate addition to a Paul Revere Mall in the North End could there be than a statue of the famous midnight rider? Accordingly, a bronze equestrian statue, originally modelled by Cyrus E. Dallin in 1885, was cast and placed in the mall on September 22, 1940. Money for the statue came from the George Robert White Fund.

The thirties also saw the first successful Italian efforts to gain political control of their destiny. A redistricting of 1915 had placed the North, South, and West Ends together, virtually securing control of the whole area by the Irish political machine, the Hendricks Club. Italians were slow to mount opposition to this state of affairs for a variety of reasons. They were handicapped by a lack of education (the area had the lowest median education level in the city in 1930: 6.3

years of school). In addition, they harbored a distrust of politics, a distrust which was their heritage from the Old World. They also distrusted outsiders and, at times, even members of their own nationality. Traditionally, *paesani* groups distrusted other *paesani* groups, and it was a long time before this fundamental disunity could be overcome. However, the thirties saw the election of Joe Langone, Jr., to state senator (1932), Edward Bacigalupo to state representative (1934), and Joe Russo to a seat on the city council (1939).[7] The power of the Hendricks Club was waning as Italian-Americans at last made their votes count. The natural distrust of government that began in Italy, where corrupt government had been a fact of southern Italian living, had kept Italians out of the political arena long enough. Throughout the days of the depression, popular sentiment held that jobs on the WPA and other relief organizations were available only to those with political power, and North End residents had none. Finally, it became apparent that some of the injustice could be rectified by ousting those politicians who had allowed these practices to occur.

Politics was not the only concern of North Enders in the thirties. On a more mundane level, the preparation and enjoyment of food was a happy preoccupation of North Enders. Famous people came to sample the cuisine of the area, already building its reputation for fine Italian cookery; and no celebrity was more welcome in the little restaurants than the great Italian opera star Enrico Caruso, who never failed to visit the North End when he was in Boston. One of his favorite restaurants was said to be the Grotto Azura at 294 Hanover Street. Another was the Posillipo Restaurant which reopened as Felicia's in 1954. An amusing anecdote is told of one visit to Boston. Attempting to cash a check, Caruso could find no way to prove his identity. The teller insisted on some confirmation that he was, indeed, Enrico Caruso. After a few moments thought, Caruso began to sing. When the "Celeste Aida" filled the air, there could be no doubt about who the man was, and the check was promptly cashed!

The forties, like the thirties, were a quiet time in the North End. Again, war broke out and the neighborhood joined the rest of the nation in supporting the war effort. As in World War I, many North End men served in various branches of the armed forces. Soldiers were stationed at the Christopher Columbus School on Tileston Street, which was temporarily converted to a barracks. Their primary duty was to help unload needed supplies at the waterfront, but many residents remember hours that the soldiers spent drilling to be ready for possible combat.

All during this time the area continued to be known as a poverty-stricken one. According to the 1940 census, 16.46% of the dwelling units were in need of major repairs. More than 60% of the buildings were 40 or more years old. Houses were, in general, substandard and overcrowded. Even though the population had shrunk to 17,598, the population density was an incredible 924.3 persons per acre.[8] The community had to deal with the special problems caused by these conditions if it wished to remain a neighborhood. Significant numbers of its younger second-generation residents were leaving for suburban communities.

One of the North End's assets was a willingness of the people to try and improve their situation. All through the 40's and 50's efforts were made to improve youth facilities in order to offset the problems that could occur when idle teenagers were left to find their own amusement. The North Bennet Street Industrial School and the Union both continued their programs. The North End Branch Library sponsored a dynamic teen council. In 1946 puppet shows — now a long-standing North End tradition — were begun in the library. The marionette shows were the idea of Mary U. Nichols, North End Librarian. While she organized this program, all the work was done by neighborhood children, who eagerly competed for the chance to perform in the productions. Youngsters flocked to the weekly shows, usually held on Saturday mornings, to see such favorites as "Hansel and Gretel" or "Pinocchio" come to life. Miss Nichols lived to direct only a few years of the puppet programs, but the tradition has been continued by subsequent children's librarians. Sadness at her untimely death in 1949 led to the establishment of an award in her memory. The Mary U. Nichols book prize is awarded each year to a North End boy and a North End girl in their final year of study at Christopher Columbus and Julie Billiart High Schools for excellence in English.

Before 1945 there had been no local high school in the North End. Public school pupils attended the Eliot Grammar School and then the Michelangelo School, opened in 1919, for their junior high years. Parochial students attended St. Anthony's, St. John's, and St. Mary's. For high school, they left the North End. In 1945 this deficiency was partially overcome with the establishment of Christopher Columbus High School for boys, staffed by the Franciscan Fathers, and Julie Billiart High School for girls, staffed by the Sisters of Notre Dame de Namur. The schools were located in the former Columbus Grammar School building. Bishop Mazzarella served as director of Columbus High School in 1944, before its formal opening as a high school. Christopher Columbus draws students from all over Boston. Julie Billiart has a student body composed primarily of North End girls. When the Sisters of Notre Dame left the North End upon the closure of St. Mary's School in 1973, they also ceased their association with Julie Billiart, and responsibility for the school passed to the Salesian Sisters.

The first director of Christopher Columbus, Bishop Mazzarella, is another example of a North End boy who rose by hard work and determination to a position of great accomplishment in his chosen field. Born in Italy, he came to the North End as a young orphan to live with his sister and her family. Like so many others, he attended the Eliot School. After attending Boston College High School, he determined on a vocation in the priesthood, entered the Franciscan order, and was ordained a priest in 1931. He served in several different assignments before returning to head Christopher Columbus High School for a year in 1944-45. Finding his life's work was elsewhere, he became a missionary priest in Honduras and in 1957 returned home to Boston for the ceremony raising him to the position of Bishop in Honduras.

Another North Ender also made a surprising contribution to society. Born in the North End in 1863, John Deferrari began work as a fruit merchant. The business prospered. From this small beginning he went on to make a fortune in real estate and in the stock market. All through these years he was a devoted user of the Boston Public Library and as he grew old, he determined to repay the library for the service he had received. In 1947 he announced the formation of a foundation to give one million dollars to the library. This gift helped build the new addition in Copley Square. The main hall of the new building was named Deferrari Hall to commemorate his contribution. His family home on Wesley Place is located directly behind the North End Branch of the library which he helped so greatly.

In the fifties the North End continued to seek opportunities for its children. It also began to feel the effects of urban renewal and change, with some good and some unfortunate results. Finally, its image as a haven of crime was both refuted and given a boost. All these factors interacted in the North End thirty years ago, and many of their after-effects are still a major concern of North Enders today.

Recreational activities for children were a prime concern for North End parents, as they had been in the 40's. The Christopher Columbus Catholic Center was planned to provide athletic facilities for all the youth of the area. The gym was also made available to Christopher Columbus and Julie Billiart students, who had no facilities of their own. It was formally opened in October 1951. Besides the gymnasium, an auditorium, meeting room, and arts and crafts room were made available to the neighborhood children.

North End parents recognized that their children needed even more recreational facilities. When swimming at the old beach was banned due to the rising bacterial count in Boston harbor, it became obvious that the North End youngsters could greatly benefit from the installation of a pool. The pool was proposed in 1950 and dedicated in June 1952.

The result of North End concern for their children, an extension of traditional Italian family closeness, succeeded in making the North End an area of extremely low juvenile delinquency. The district had developed a stigma in the 20's and 30's due to the problems caused by prohibition and the joblessness of the depression. In the eyes of many

The next generation of North Enders — will there still be a community for them?

outsiders the North End was a dangerous city slum inhabited by a criminal element. These people were surprised to discover that in more affluent suburbs the juvenile delinquency problem was much worse than in the crowded, poor North End. At a time when juvenile delinquency had begun to rise to the point of being a national problem, the North End was constantly lowering its delinquency rates. In 1938 there were 118 cases of breaking and entering, shoplifting, and larceny involving juveniles in the area. In 1951 there were only 20 cases in the whole North End. This record was maintained throughout the fifties. The North End in 1958 accounted for less than 1% of the juvenile delinquency figures in Boston.[9] Unfortunately, spectacular robberies like the Brinks robbery in 1950 at the foot of Prince Street helped erase this glowing record in outsiders' eyes. The robbery was not committed by North Enders, and the North End was not responsible for the daring act, but the two became associated in the national coverage accorded this event. Local residents were so upset, that when a flim crew later arrived to shoot a movie on the robbery in the North End, they protested this unfair depiction of their area of the city.

The image of the North End as a slum led people to consider it a prime candidate for the urban renewal projects contemplated in the fifties. The first project to cause a tremendous upheaval was the proposed central artery. Boston's traffic pattern was chaotic in the area, and it seemed obvious that some solution should be sought. Regrettably, the solution caused many other problems. First, the isolation of the North End from the rest of Boston, always a distinction of the area, was reemphasized in steel and concrete. A genuine physical barrier sliced the historic and residential landmark from the main city. Also, more than 100 dwellings were destroyed and 900 businesses uprooted. North End wholesalers organized a "Save Boston Business" Committee to protest the imminent skyway. A "Committee To Save the North End of Boston," organized in April 1950, held mass meetings protesting what they felt would result in an increased deterioration of their area. However, protests were too late and never sufficiently organized. In November the first 54 plots of land were taken on Haverhill, Beverly, and Traverse Streets. In February 1951 one resident complained, "We've heard rumors that these buildings would be torn down since last summer, but we hoped it wasn't true."[10] Protest erupted again when residents learned in October that Hanover Street, the main thoroughfare, would be cut off. The famed Post Office was threatened, and pushcart peddlers on Blackstone Street faced eviction. All protests were ineffective, however, and the expressway was built. Almost as soon as it was finished, discussion began about the feasability of sinking the structure, which is an eyesore in the center of Boston. Various plans have been proposed and discarded, but the subject is never dropped for long. Today, in 1975 the controversy has again surfaced, over 20 years after the expressway was built.

The residents themselves were aware of the condition of their area and in the 50's they began to organize to change things. The narrow streets of the North End were not well suited to modern garbage collection methods. On Salem Street, particularly, left-over fruits and vegetables were rotting on the streets, creating a health hazard and an unsightly appearance. In February 1950 a meeting was held at the North End Union to ask the city for better refuse disposal. The North End Rehabilitation and Conservation Commission was inaugurated in 1955 to spearhead plans for a cleaner, more modern North End. Joseph Campana, director of the Credit Union, headed the group. Faced with the expressway and the razing of the West End, the residents felt that they would soon be dislocated for a massive urban renewal program. A few houses were taken for the new tunnel in 1959, but by and large the North End arrived in the 60's intact.

To write about events of the last 15 years becomes difficult because, even more than for the 50's, the events of the 60's and 70's are part of an ongoing process of change that has still not been resolved. The North End at the beginning of the 60's was a self-sufficient neighborhood still overwhelmingly Italian in ethnic composition. 30%

of the 4,300 dwelling units were classified as deteriorating and 5% as dilapidated, but the area had escaped the total renewal program that had annihilated neighboring West End. [11] The area looked poor, but had a very low welfare case load and crime rate. As some of the advantages of life in the North End became known, people began to look on the district in a new light. They began to see beyond the surface of crowded, not always well-cleaned streets and alleys, the old houses, the lack of physical space. What they saw was a community of people who helped each other through emergencies. It was the type of neighborhood in which, when fire destroyed a dwelling, neighbors and relatives took in the victims and found shelter and clothing for them.

In the middle of the city the streets were crowded at night. Unlike most urban areas, people could walk safely after dark. The ambience of the Italian way of life, visible in the small cafes and restaurants, the fruit stands and open markets, the gatherings of elderly in the Prado and young men in the park — all this was finally recognized as a way of life to be emulated by rushed and frantic Americans. Jane Jacobs, in her classic study, *The Death and Life of Great American Cities*, gave the North End national prominence as a model of city life. In response to Jane Jacob's publicity, Boston Redevelopment Authority officials acknowledged the North End as "one of the most lively neighborhoods of Boston" [12] and assured residents that no West-End-like destruction of the community would occur. This prominence became a challenge to the North End. The need for some renewal was apparent to all. Further deterioration of the neighborhood could reactivate calls for major renewal. North Enders became aware of the image they now presented to the world. Tourists and local Bostonians were descending on the area, not just to view the historical buildings, but eager to sample this paragon of community living. In the 60's, then, a period of self-renewal — still ongoing — began. Cardinal Cushing restored St. Stephen's in 1965. In the same year the old North End Branch Library was replaced by a beautiful modern structure at 25 Parmenter Street. Designed by Carl Koch Associates, the building sought to re-create the atmosphere of an Italian piazza. Individual North Enders took advantage of the rising prosperity of the 60's to undertake their own renewal projects to upgrade private property. A plan to close the Michelangelo School in 1963 was squashed by determined neighborhood opposition. Needed repairs were obtained to enable the school to function as an educational institution.

The discovery of the North End by outsiders had unexpected and — for the North Enders — unsettling, disturbing results. Taking advantage of the low rents and physical safety, young working people and professionals, attracted by the opportunity to experience a new style of city life, began to move into the area. As this influx continued and property was upgraded, North End families came into competition with the new wave of settlers for good housing. Some people naturally resented what they saw as a threat to their cohesiveness and close, stable neighborhood life. Friendly on the surface, they feared a loss of identity as their homogeneity was lessened. They saw this influx as a more subtle way of breaking up the North End community than the wrecker's ball, but just as effective. Large-scale renewal of the waterfront was also a cause of tension. The new luxury stores and apartments contemplated were an economic asset to the city and to the North End. But where were the poor and elderly to go?

Concurrent with the arrival of the American professionals, a change in immigration laws (1965) resulted in a new migration of Italian immigrants to the area. A community that seemed to be in danger of losing its ethnic identity as 2nd and 3rd-generation children grew up ignorant of the language of their parents and grandparents found its streets once again filled with newly-arrived settlers whose language was Italian. A population that had been getting progressively older (with 54.3% of its population over 35) [13] received a new group of immigrant children to bolster declining school populations.

A final factor in recent North End history is a disturbing one. Even the North End, with its tradition of family closeness, was not immune to the upheavals of the 60's, particularly the rebellion of youth. Vandalism increased and by the late 60's and 70's the North End was facing some of the problems with drugs and alcohol that other com-

A small intimate neighborhood in a growing, changing Boston. How will it meet the challenge of the future?

munities had faced earlier. In the early 60's so-called "hippies" were discouraged from living in the North End. By the late 60's North End teenages had accepted some of the styles of the prevalent youth culture. As they identified with their peers throughout the country, some values that were held by their parents and grandparents were rejected. North End parents were faced with alienation, boredom, and an increase in drug use and were not prepared, at first, to deal with this new phenomenon.

So the North End entered the 70's poised at yet another crossroads in its long and varied history. The old ethnic community still has an amazing vigor. It gains strength from the new Italian immigrants who continue to cross the Atlantic as immigrants have done for hundreds of years. Of course, these modern immigrants frequently make the trip by airplane in a couple of hours, rather than spend weeks cramped in the miserable hold of a slow steamer. As long as they continue to come, the North End will have a chance to retain the atmosphere that is its distinctive hallmark.

At the same time the area will continue to attract people of other backgrounds who are interested in sharing its way of life. The danger of this migration of fashionable residents swamping the North End will be an integral part of the story of the next 10 years. However, change has always been an attribute of the North End. In 300 years, Puritans, Blacks, Royalists, Irish, Jews, and Portuguese have also been North Enders. Perhaps the Italian community will one day leave the North End, and perhaps this is inevitable. For many, Americanization has already led to assimilation into the larger community. While many North Enders have chosen to stay, others have left, seeking advantages that the North End, with all its charms, cannot provide. Perhaps the next 10 years will see a new breed of North Enders.

And perhaps the two groups will be able to work together to provide a bright future for the North End. They are all united by a common desire to live here. Those new residents who sought out the North End for its neighborhood closeness should be equally reluctant to see this closeness disappear. There are problems in the North End, as there are in every community. There is still a need for further renewal, for more play area, for more constructive activities for youth. Yet there is so much worth preserving in these old streets that it would be an incalculable loss to the city for the North End to sacrifice its uniqueness in order to deal with these concerns. Success depends on the unselfish efforts of many people working as a community. And, if there is one distinctive trait that has characterized the North End through more than 300 years of existence, it has been its continuous sense of community. Hopefully, this will be the strength that carries it through the uncertainties of the next 300 years.

Notes — Chapter 1

[1]Robert A. Woods, *Americans in Process* (Boston: Houghton Mifflin, 1902), 11.

[2]*Ibid.*

[3]Annie Haven Thwing, *The Crooked and Narrow Streets of the Town of Boston, 1630-1822* (Boston: Marshall and Co., 1920), 23.

[4]"Copp's Hill" *Boston Post Magazine*, February 27, 1949.

[5]Work was completed in 1804. Michael and Susan Southworth, *Boston 200 Discovery Network: North End Survey* (Boston: unpub, n.d.). Reproductions of a brochure issued by St. Stephen's Church.

[6] The church is though to be St. Andrew's-by-the-wardrobe in the Blackfriars section of London. It was destroyed in 1940.

[7]Information on the caucus was obtained from several sources including *Boston: a Close-Up of Its Neighborhoods, Its People and Its Problems* (Boston: The Boston Globe, 1971) and Rev. Edward G. Porter, *Rambles in Old Boston* (Boston: A.M. Thayer and Co., 1890).

[8]Porter, 95.

[9]Southworth. Reproduction of a plaque on the building.

[10] Woods, 30.

Notes — Chapter 2

[1]*Boston: The Official Bicentennial Handbook* (New York: E.P. Dutton, 1975).

[2]Southworth reproduces an article claiming that the Dodds were the last old family in the North End. Woods, 34, cites the Beecher home on Sheafe Street as the last home to be abandoned by the aristocrats.

[3]Woods, 41.

[4]*Ibid*, 62. Also reproduced in Southworth.

[5]Southworth. Reproduction of a newspaper article by George Weston, Jr.

[6]Woods, 74.

[7]Oscar Handlin, *Boston's Immigrants*, rev. ed. (Cambridge, Mass.: Harvard University Press, 1959), 91-95.

[8]The decline of the area around North Street is mentioned in many sources including: George Weston, Jr., *Boston Ways: High, By, and Folk*, 3rd. ed. (Boston: Beacon Press, 1974), 182; John Galvin, "Boston's First Irish Cop" *Boston Magazine*, v. 67 no. 3 (March 1975), 52-55 + ; and Southworth.

[9] Galvin, 52-55 + .

[10] Handlin discusses the pecularities of the political situation of the 50's and 60's fully in his book.

[11] Galvin, 52-55 + .

[12] Material obtained from several sources including *This is the North End* (Boston: The Italian News Publishing Co., 1956) unpaged; and a booklet prepared by the church for its 100th anniversary.

[13] Samuel Adams Drake, *Old Landmarks and Historic Personages of Boston* (Boston: Osgood and Co., 1875), 223-4.

[14] Newspaper clipping from North End files undated.

[15] William Whyte, "Race Conflicts in the North End of Boston," *The New England Quarterly*, v. 12 (December 1939), 623-642 and Warren Phillips, *Boston's North End Italians: A Study of Their Immigration, Settlement and Society, 1895-1920* (unpublished paper, 1975).

[16] The Portuguese are briefly discussed in R.H. Lord, *History of the Archdiocese of Boston*, 3 vols. (New York: Sheed and Ward, 1944), Volume 3, Chapter 9 "The Coming of the Newer Catholic Races."

Notes — Chapter 3

[1] Richard Gambino, *Blood of My Blood: The Dilemma of the Italian Americans* (Garden City, New York: Doubleday, 1974) devotes a great deal of space to an examination of the reasons for immigration from italy.

[2] Walter Firey, *Land Use in Central Boston* (New York: Greenwood Press, 1968), 181 and Wood, 41.

[3] The most complete source on the Jewish community in the North End is Arnold A. Weider, *The Early Jewish Community of Boston's North End* (Waltham, Mass.: Brandeis University, 1962).

[4] Firey, 184.

[5] Phillips, 4ff.

[6] *Ibid.* and Woods, 40.

[7] Woods.

[8] Phillips, 17.

[9] Firey, 215.

[10] Phillips, 13ff.

[11] *Ibid.*, 20. General information on work that the immigrants obtained is also in Robert Foerster, *The Italian Emigration of Our Times* (New York: Arno Press, 1969).

[12] Southworth. Reproduction of a newspaper article by Pietrina Maravigna.

[13] Phillips, 20.

[14] Undated newspaper clippings and Phillips, 21.

[15] *This is the North End.*

[16] *Ibid.* Also Lord, Volume 3, Chapter 9.

[17] Newspaper clippings from files and scrapbooks.

[18] *Ibid.*

[19] Information on the North Bennet Street Industrial School and the North End Union obtained from newspaper articles and scrapbooks.

[20] Rajinder S. Walia, *The North End: A Survey of Its Community and The Branch Library* (unpublished dissertation, Simmons School of Library Science, May 1967), 42.

[21] *Ibid.*, 29 and *This is The North End, passim.*

Notes — Chapter 4

[1] Correspondence from Mrs. Catherine Cirignano, 38 Sheafe Street, North End resident.

[2] Phillips, 10.

[3] Whyte, 640ff.

[4] *Boston Evening Transcript*, October 5, 1927.

[5] Firey, 200.

[6] Southworth.

[7] Whyte, 639 and Firey, 188.

[8] Firey, 172.

[9] Southworth and newspaper accounts.

[10] Newspaper clippings.

[11] *Boston: A Close-Up . . .*

[12] Newspaper clipping.

[13] Walia, 17.

Bibliography

Action for Boston Community Development. *The Educational Experience of East Boston and the North End: a preliminary report,* by Richard Cohen. Boston, June 16, 1971.

Sketch of socio-economic conditions in East Boston and the North End with special attention to their effect on the education of children of Italian ancestry.

Action for Boston Community Development and United Community Services of Metropolitan Boston. *Five Ethnic Groups in Boston: Blacks, Irish, Italians, Greeks and Puerto Ricans: a joint report,* ed. by Charles M. Sullivan. June 1972.

Comprehensive tables were prepared on all facets of daily life — general characteristics, education, income, religion, employment, attitudes about self and others, residential mobility and urbanization.

Action for Boston Community Development. *Socio-economic Characteristics of Boston Neighborhoods: Data from the 1970 U.S. Census,* prepared by Charles M. Sullivan. Boston, November 1, 1972.

Statistical evaluation of each of Boston's neighborhoods.

Bailyn, Bernard. *The Ordeal of Thomas Hutchinson.* Cambridge, Mass., Harvard University Press, 1974.

Prize-winning biography not only explores the personality of Hutchinson, but provides much valuable insight into the Loyalists in Boston before and during the Revolution.

Barr, Vilma "The Haymarket Affair," *Yankee* (November 1970), 92-98 + .

Description of Boston's Haymarket and discussion of its future amid talk of renewal.

Boston: A Close-Up of Its Neighborhoods, Its People and Its Problems. Boston, The Boston Globe, (1971).

A series of articles on different neighborhoods collected in one volume. The North End chapter is a brief outline of population, atmosphere, some historical data and general comments.

Boston Herald Traveler Research Department. *Boston: America's Sixth Market: 1950 Census.* Boston, October 18, 1954.

Population figures for North End, Orient Heights and East Boston. Notes decline of the North End's population, percent of populace with central heat, T.V., refrigerators, etc.

Boston Redevelopment Authority Planning Department. *North End Recreation and Open Space Study,* prepared for the Parks and Recreation Department, Spring 1968.

A study of population, housing and land use; an inventory of the existing supply of recreation and open space facilities; an analysis of the adequacy and need for facilities; and a preliminary plan.

Boston: The Official Bicentennial Handbook, ed. by Cleveland Amory. New York, E. P. Dutton and Company, 1975.

Facts and legends of North End landmarks and monuments are briefly included.

Brindisi, R. "The Italian and Public Health." *Charities*, v. 12 (1904), 483-504.

A study of the health of Italian immigrants in Boston. Cited favorably were sobriety, endurance, and sound diet. Mortality rates, although low, were shown to be affected by the rigors of slum life and the immigrants' distrust of hospitals. Rickets and tuberculosis, particularly, were on the increase.

Bruner, J. and Sayre, J. "Shortwave Listening in an Italian Community: Study of Boston's Italian North End." *Public Opinion Quarterly*, v. 5, no. 4 (December 1941), 640-656.

This study may have been prompted by fears about the loyalty of the Italian-American in World War II. While it was found that many North Enders listened to Italian radio programs, and shortwave listening was linked to "militant" Italianism, extreme Italian nationalists were a distinct minority of the population.

Bushee, Frederick A. "Italian Immigrants in Boston." *Arena*, v. 17 (April 1897), 722-734.

At the time of his study Bushee counted approximately 18,000 Italian immigrants in Boston, mainly single men. The padrone system is discussed, also occupations, social habits, reactions to the Catholic Church in America.

Carlevale, Joseph Williams. *Leading Americans of Italian Descent in Massachusetts*. Plymouth, Mass., The Memorial Press, 1946.

Short biographies of 4,000 Italian-Americans who have made contributions to Massachusetts life in diverse fields.

"Character of Italian Immigration." *New England Magazine*, n.s. 35 (1906), 216-220.

Feels that Italian immigration is a dangerous problem. The Italians are "from races not suited to our civilization," and "radically different from us in education, habits of life, and institutions of government."

Crawford, Mary Caroline. *Old Boston in Colonial Days*. Boston, the Page Company, 1908.

Biographical approach to the history of Boston containing material on the Mathers, Sir Henry Frankland and others.

Davidson, Bill. "The Mafia: How it Bleeds New England." *Saturday Evening Post*, v. 240 (November 18, 1967), 27-31.

Popularized "history" of the Mafia wars in New England.

Davis, W.H. "The Relation of the Foreign Population to the Mortality Rates of Boston," a paper read at the 37th annual meeting of the American Academy of Medicine, June 1912.

Breakdowns of the death rates from various diseases by nationality and some general conclusions about the relative health of the various immigrant groups.

Dictionary of American Biography. Ed. by Allen Johnson. New York, Scribners, 1927, 1955.

Concise, scholarly accounts of the lives of famous North Enders such as Paul Revere, Governor Hutchinson, Judge Samuel Sewall, the Mathers and others.

diGiovanni, Norman Thomas. "Tenements and Cadillacs: Boston's Italian Quarter." *Nation*, 187 (December 13, 1958), 443-445.

A sympathetic view of the North End by an author who is himself a North End resident.

Dogherty, Marian A. *'Scusa Me Teacher*. Francestown, N.H., Marshall Jones, 1943.

Reminiscences of a teacher at the North End's Hancock School during the period when the Jewish community was still large, but the Italian community was constantly growing.

Drake, Samuel Adams. *Old Boston Taverns and Tavern Clubs*. Boston, W.A. Butterfield, 1917, reprinted Detroit, Singing Tree Press, 1971.

History of various colonial taverns including the North End's famous "Green Dragon" and "Salutation Tavern," among others.

Drake, Samuel Adams. *Old Landmarks and Historic Personages of Boston*. Boston, J. R. Osgood, 1874.

Through description of various buildings and locales in Boston, Adams' book provides much anecdotal history about the colonial North End.

Dunn, Elizabeth and Sheila Elfman. *Four Areas of Boston, 1970*. United Community Services of Metropolitan Boston, 1973.

Analyzes 1970 census data for population and family composition among other socio-economic characteristics.

Firey, Walter. *Land Use in Central Boston*. New York, Greenwood Press, 1968. Chapter V. "The Influence of Localized Social Solidarity Upon Land Use: The North End," 170-225.

At a time when the North End was still considered an undesirable slum, Firey brought together statistics and personal observations to prove that the Italian community existed, not just because its people could not afford to live elsewhere, but as a positive affirmation of a value system stressing ethnic solidarity and the continuance of Italian custom that the people wished to preserve.

Fleming, Thomas. "Paul Revere, He Went That-aWay." *Yankee* (April 1975), 94-103 + .

Interesting tales about one of the North End's most famous residents.

Foerster, Robert. *The Italian Emigration of Our Times.* New York, Arno Press, 1969.

References to Boston are scattered, but the book is nevertheless a good source for general information on immigration, containing statistics on employment, housing, infant mortality, etc.

Galvin, John. "Boston's First Irish Cop." *Boston Magazine,* v 67, no. 3 (March 1975), 52-55 + .

Story of Barney McGinniskin, Irish North Ender, with an insert describing the notorious Ann Street (now North) brothel district of the 19th century.

Gambino, Richard. *Blood of My Blood: the dilemma of the Italian-Americans.* Garden City, New York, Doubleday, 1974.

An examination of the Italian heritage and its transformations in adjusting to the ways of the New World. Explanation of the economic and social forces in Italy that caused the great immigration which began in the 1880's.

Guy, Don. "There are Two Ways To Ring the Bells of the Old North Church." *Yankee* (October 1974), 72-78 + .

The bells of the Old North Church, designed to ring free, have been in fixed position for many years for fear of damaging the church structure. Bicentennial planners were interested in the possibility of restoring them to usher in the 200th celebrations.

Handlin, Oscar. *Boston's Immigrants.* Rev. ed. Cambridge, Mass., Harvard University Press, 1959.

Acclaimed study of the Irish immigration into Boston in the 19th century and its effects on the immigrants and on the society which they were thrown into.

Howells, William Dean. *Suburban Sketches.* Boston, J.R. Osgood and Co., 1872.

In Chapter 2, "Doorstep Acquaintance," Howells discusses Italians in the Boston area before the great immigration. Most of these early immigrants were northern Italians. The author advances some interesting opinions about the character of the immigrants, attesting that they are lazy, but lively and amiable;

some are shiftless, but on the whole they are more desirable than the "dark-mooded, sad-faced men" from the south of Italy.

Jacobs, Jane. *The Death and Life of Great American Cities.* New York, Random House, 1961.

The now classic study of urban America that cites the North End favorably as a livable urban neighborhood. A pattern of social organization that involves the people in street life and each other's personal safety makes North End streets far safer than other cities' streets.

Jacobs, Jane. "How City Planners Hurt Cities." *Saturday Evening Post* (October 14, 1961), 12-14.

Short article mentioning the healthy atmosphere of North End life compared to disasters caused by city planners who imposed their theories on neighborhoods.

Jacobs, Jane. "Violence in the City Streets." *Harpers Magazine* (September 1961), 37-43.

Published just prior to her book (see above), the article is a convenient summary of many of the ideas that she develops in *The Death and Life of Great American Cities.*

Judge, Joseph. "Those Proper and Other Bostonians." *National Geographic* (September 1974), 352-380.

Several pages of text describe North End's atmosphere, plus color photographs of the feasts.

Leach, Joseph. *Bright Particular Star: the life and times of Charlotte Cushman.* New Haven, Conn., Yale University Press. 1970.

Biography of North End resident (born on Parmenter Street) who became one of America's leading 19th century actresses.

"Little Italy in the Streets of Paul Revere." *Independent*, v. 114 (June 20, 1925), 693-696.

Photographic essay containing nine photos. Description of traditional Italian funeral led by a band.

Lord, R.H. *History of the Archdiocese of Boston.* 3 vols. New York, Sheed and Ward, 1944. Volume III, Chapter 9, "The Coming of the Newer Catholic Races."

Discusses the organization of Catholic churches for the Portuguese and the Italians in the North End.

Massachusetts Historical Society. *Thomas Hutchinson and His Contemporaries.* Boston, 1974.

Brief biographical text accompanies reproductions of portraits and pertinent documents of the period.

Massachusetts. *Report of the Commissioner on Immigration.* Boston, 1914.

Statistics on number of Italians of foreign birth in Massachusetts 1850-1910. They show the spectacular rise in the population after 1880.

McCord, David. *About Boston.* Boston, Little, Brown and Co., 1948, 1973.

Short essay (pages 85-90) describing the Italian atmosphere of the area and noting some of the colonial landmarks.

Moffat, Adeline. "Exhibition of Italian arts and crafts in Boston." *Survey,* v. 22 (1909), 51-53.

Description of an exhibition held in Boston to locate able craftsmen of Italian ancestry in the Greater Boston area. Book illuminating, wood carving, embroidery and lace-making featured.

Phillips, Warren. *Boston's North End Italians: A Study of Their Immigration, Settlement and Society, 1895-1920.* Unpublished thesis, 30p., 1975.

Uses statistics compiled from government documents and rare sources to discuss fully the character of the settlers in the early period of massive Italian immigration.

Porter, Rev. Edward G. *Rambles in Old Boston.* Boston, Cripples, Upham and Company, 1886.

Much historical and anecdotal information on the North End's colonial buildings and landmarks.

Riso, Don. "Along the Torrone Trail." *Boston Magazine* (November 1974), 110-116.

A tour of the pastry stores of the North End.

Schofield, William G. *Freedom by the Bay.* New York, Rand McNally, 1974.

History and anecdotes about Freedom Trail sites are related with humor. Paul Revere's House, Old North Church, Faneuil Hall and general information about the North End are also included.

Scudder, Vida D. "Experiments in Fellowship: Work with Italians in Boston." *The Survey,* v. 22 (1909), 47-51.

Explores the feelings of the immigrants about their new life in America. Many saw the change to American life as economically good, but morally bad.

Shagouty, Charles, M.D. "The Molasses Disaster." *Boston Sunday Herald,* January 9, 1966.

North End's worst disaster occurred when the molasses tank exploded in 1919.

Simmonds, D. C. "Anti-Italian-American Riddles in New England." *Journal of American Folklore*, v. 79 (July 1966), 475-478.

Anti-Italian jokes rise as the social and economic aspirations of the group place them in competition with others.

Snyder, Wendy. *Haymarket.* Cambridge, Mass., MIT Press, 1970.

A photographic essay of the market district and the people who live and work there.

Solomon, Barbara Miller. *Ancestors and Immigrants: A Changing New England Tradition,* Cambridge, Mass., Harvard University Press, 1956.

Overview of the changes in Boston society as the Irish immigrants settled in the city and sought political power.

Southworth, Michael and Susan. *Boston 200 Discovery Network: North End Survey.* privately published, undated.

Designed for the use of the Boston 200 Committee, this handy compilation of material from many sources covers the North End from colonial times to the present day.

"This Is the North End." Boston, The Italian News Publishing Company, 1956.

Compilation of 25 articles, each highlighting one aspect of the North End community. Includes material on the churches, organizations, historical landmarks, etc.

Thwing, Annie Haven. *The Crooked and Narrow Streets of the Town of Boston,* 1630-1822. Boston, Marshall Jones and Company, 1920. Chapter I, "The North End," 26-78.

Colonial and early 19th century North End lore described in a tour through its ancient streets.

Tramontozzi, Linda. "Boston's North End, My Home Town." *Yankee* (September 1971), 68-75 +

The North End's uniqueness in America: a strong European heritage in a Yankee setting. The article particularly stresses the low level of violence and juvenile delinquency in the area.

Tramontozzi, Linda. "Can Italian Power Save the North End?" *Boston Magazine* (October 1971), 56-71.

Expressed the fear that the North End would be overwhelmed by outsiders and supported the efforts of the community to protect itself.

Walia, Rajinder S. "The North End: A Survey of the Community and the Branch Library." unpub. paper, Simmons College School of Library Science (May 1967).

Comprehensive analysis of the North End of the 60's and the role of the North End Branch Library in the community.

Weston, George F., Jr. *Boston Ways: High, By and Folk*, 3rd ed. Boston, Beacon Press, 1974.

Charming vignettes of Boston, primarily colonial, but also describing generally the atmosphere today.

Whitehill, Walter Muir. *Boston: A Topographical History*, 2nd ed. Cambridge, Mass., Harvard University Press, 1968.

Invaluable information for everyone wishing to imagine what the North End was shaped like 200 to 300 years ago.

Whyte, William. "Race Conflicts in the North End of Boston." *The New England Quarterly*, v. 12 (December 1939), 623-642.

The progress of the Italian immigration into the North End is detailed through diagrams. Irish-Italo tension, the effects of prohibition on racketeering, and the growth of political power are covered.

Whyte, William *Street Corner Society*. Chicago, University of Chicago Press, 1943.

This classic study of the North End social structure concentrates primarily on street corner gangs, their college-bound contemporaries, and the racketeer overlords. Names of various organizations are disguised but easily recognizable to those with a knowledge of the North End in the 30's.

Wieder, Arnold A. *The Early Jewish Community of Boston's North End*. Waltham, Mass. Brandeis University Press, 1962.

Social and community organization, employment and the role of religion are all treated fully in this study of the Jewish community.

Woods, Amy. "Italians of New England." *New England Magazine*, n.s. 30 (1904), 626-32.

In this anti-Italian article Miss Woods expressed fear that Italians would never adjust or assimilate with the other citizens of their new country.

Woods, Robert A. *Americans in Process*. Boston, Houghton Mifflin and Company, 1902.

This turn-of-the-century, brief history of the North End covers the different ethnic groups and their sections of the area. Attention is given to the people, their occupations, problems, religious affiliations, frictions with other ethnic groups, and other sociological concerns.

Woods, Robert A. "Notes on Italians in Boston," *The Survey*, v. 12 (May 7, 1904), 451-452.

Advocates sending Italians into the countryside to relieve city slums. Concludes that Italians are generally desirable immigrants.

In addition to the titles mentioned above, a large portion of the information obtained for use for this study came from the newspaper files of the North End Branch Library, scrapbooks of newspaper clippings made available by John Dexter of North Bennet Street Industrial School, and other clippings saved by Pietrina Maravigna of the North End.